FRUIT
&
VEGETABLE
JUICE THERAPY

By
N.N. Saha

An imprint of
B. Jain Publishers (P) Ltd.
USA — Europe — India

FRUIT AND VEGETABLE JUICE THERAPY

6th Impression: 2015

All rights reserved. No part of this book may be reproduced, stored in a retrieval system or transmitted, in any form or by any means, mechanical, photocopying, recording or otherwise, without any prior written permission of the publisher.

© with the Publisher

Published by Kuldeep Jain for

HEALTH HARMONY

An imprint of

B. Jain Publishers (P) Ltd.
1921/10, Chuna Mandi, Paharganj, New Delhi 110 055 (INDIA)
Tel.: +91-11-4567 1000 • *Fax:* +91-11-4567 1010
Email: info@bjain.com *Website:* **www.bjain.com**

Printed in India

ISBN: 978-81-319-0604-0

PREFACE

The drug is not the way to good health but it is the way to further disease. Drugs usually cause temporary relief from any disease. Constant consumption of drugs may develop side-effect or after-effects in the body. Supposed pain-killers like anacin, aspirin, novalgin, crocin, analgin, etc. may give temporary relief from pain but they will surely cause a permanent damage to the heart, liver and kidneys. A more serious disease is likely to develop later. This is a serious drawback of using drugs. Many people have been suffering from white patches all over the skin due to excess use of antibiotics. This is a permanent defect.

It would be better if you follow natural ways to health. You should take food as nature has made it, i.e. raw fruits and vegetables. It refers to 'Food as it grows'. This is the best food for human beings. Scientists have found that cooking destroys most of the natural vitamins and minerals.

It has been found that germs do not cause disease but the accumulation of filth, waste products or garbage inside the body invite germs to invade thereby causing disease. If there is no garbage or filth, there will be no germs, no disease. So the key-word to good health is detoxification. And detoxification of the whole body can be most effectively done by consuming raw fruit and vegetable juices in plenty.

How to select the right fruit for a specific disease? You will find its answer in this book. In case of acute dysentery, if you take a glass of musumbi juice and a few cloves of fried garlics in the morning for 4/5 days, you will get adequate relief from it. In case of fevers, if you take a glass of orange juice and a few cloves of fried garlic, you will surely get instant relief. In old age, you can't keep your health fit by drugs. But if you take a few cloves of fried garlic and a glass of musumbi or lemon juice daily, you will be able to keep yourself fit and active. If your health remains fit, active and healthy, you can work more, earn more, enjoy more, live in this beautiful world for longer periods.

P-95, Unique Park,   **N.N. SAHA**
Behala,
Calcutta - 700 034

CONTENTS

	Page No.
Fruit	1
What is meant by the term 'vegetable'	1
Distinction between fruits and vegetables	2
Fruits and Vegetables — their importance	2
Vegetables that are usually consumed in their raw state	3
Classification of fruits	3
Classification of vegetables	5
Chief causes of diseases and their remedies	7
Eat your food the way God made it	10
Overconsumption or obesity	13
Drug is not the restorer of good health but means of further disease	15
Cooked food is dangerous	16
The Fruits and Vegetables	20
Garlic (Rashun/Lahsan)	21
Lemon (Lebu/Nimbu)	27
Chebulic myrobalan (Haritaki)	39
Emblic myrobalan (Amlaki)	41
Onion (Piyaj)	43
Margosa (Nim, neem)	47
Bitter-gourd (Karela)	49
Orange (Kamala lebu)	50
Papaya (Papita, penpe)	51
Marmelos/wood-apple (Bel)	54
Tomato (Bilati begun)	55
Tamarind (Imli/tentul)	58
Parbal (Patal)	60
Cucumber (Sasha, Khirika)	61
Apple (Apel)	62

Pineapple (Anaras)	63
Banana (Kela, Kala)	65
Beet	66
Carrot (Gajar)	68
Soyabean	69
Coconut (Narikel, nariyel)	70
Cashew nut (Kaju-badam)	72
Pomegranate (Dalim)	72
Cherry	75
Dates (Khejur)	75
Grape-fruit or Shaddock (Batabi lebu)	77
Lime (Musumbi)	79
Pear (Naspati)	82
Potato (Alu)	83
Guava (Peyara)	84
Watermelon (Tarmuj)	85
Lichi (Lichu)	85
Mangosteen (Gab)	86
Fig (Dumur)	87
Nutmeg jaiphal)	88
Asafoetida (Hing)	89
Walnut (Akrot)	90
Olive (Jalpai)	90
Isabgul	91
Chick-pea or gram (Chhola or chana)	92
Apricot (Khobani)	93
Currant (Karamcha, boch)	94
Peach	94
Pea-nut or ground-nut (China-badam)	95
Quince	95
Custard apple (Ata or nona)	96
Sugarcane (Akh)	97
Pea (Matar)	98
Liquorice (Jastimadhu)	98

Dandelion	99
Collard	99
Celery	100
Avocado	100
Brazil nut	101
Bread fruit	101
Plum (Kul)	102
Mango (Aam)	102
Toddy palm (Tal)	103
Wood-apple (Kath-bel)	104
Hog-plum (Amra)	104
Loquat	104
Jack-fruit (Kanthal, inchar)	105
Black-berry (Kalajam)	106
Nectarine	107
Nasturtium	107
Kumquat	108
Mandarin & Tangerine	108

The Vegetables

Spinach (Palang sak)	108
Cabbage (Bandhakapi)	110
Cauliflower (Phulkapi)	111
Egg-plant (Brinjal, Baigon)	112
Plantain (Kanchkala)	113
Beans (Sim)	114
Chilli or red pepper (Mircha, Kanchalanka)	115
Holy basil or Sacred basil (Tulsi or Tulasi)	115
Pumpkin (Lau)	116
Horse-radish/Ben oil tree (Sajne danta)	118
White pumpkin (Chal-kumro)	120
Endive	121
Acorn	122
Artichoke	122

Parsley	123
Peppermint	124
Parsnip	125
Rhubarb/Pie plant	126
Chive	126
Chervil	127
Chestnut	128
Prune	129
Pimento	129
Paprika	129
Kale	130
Gourd (Kumro)	131
Radish (Mula)	131
Lettuce	132
Leeks	134
Broccoli	135
Asparagus	136
Turnip (Salgam)	137
Okra or gumbo	138
Spearmint	138
Sorrel	139
Squash	139
Zucchini	140
Scallion	141
Dill	141
Water lily (Sapla)	142
Taro, arum (Kachu)	143
Kohlrabi	143
Marjoram	144
Chicory	144
Rutabaga	145
Fennel (Madhumika)	145
Brussels sprouts	146
Caper	147

Black pepper (Kalajira)	147
Ginger (Ada, adrak)	148
Cloves (Labanga)	149
Cardamon (Elaichi)	150
Cinnamon (Daruchini)	151
Cassava, tapioca, manioc, mandioc, yuca	152
Hickory nuts	153
Girasole or Jerusalem artichoke	153
Escarole	154
Fruit & vegetable juice formulas for specific ailments	155
Brief notes on vitamins	175
Brief notes on minerals	181
Folklore with regard to fruit juice therapy	185
Cancer	191
Heart-attack	197
High blood pressure	201
Arthritis	206
Asthma	208
Glossary of medical terms	209
Bibliography	213

DEDICATION

This book is dedicated to Shri Shri Ramkrishna Paramhansa, my spiritual master.

N.N. Saha,
Tantra Bidyamani,
Asst. Editor, Spiritual Magazine
Cuttack.

FRUIT

Fruit is the ripened ovary of a flower, either by itself or in combination with other structures that have matured with it as a unit. This botanical definition applies to both things popularly called 'fruits'; generally sweet fleshy foods such as apples, grapes, and bananas and to many things called 'vegetables', such as peas, beans and tomatoes, for these two are the products of matured ovaries.

What is meant by the term 'vegetable'

The term 'vegetable' in its broadest sense refers to any kind of plant life or plant product; it usually refers to the fresh edible portion of a herbaceous plant consumed either raw or cooked. The edible portion may be a root like a rutabaga, beet, carrot and sweet potato; a tuber or storage stem such as potato and taro; the stem as in asparagus and kohrabi; a bud such as Brussels sprouts; a bulb such as onion and garlic; a petiole or leafstock like celery and rhubarb; a leaf such as cabbage, lettuce, parsley, spinach and chive; an immature flower like cauliflower, broccoli and artichoke; a seed like pea and Lima beans; the immature fruit like brinjal (egg-plant), cucumber and sweet corn (maize) or the mature fruit like tomato and chilli.

Distinction between fruits and vegetables

Those plants or plant parts that are usually consumed with the main course of a meal are popularly regarded as vegetables; while those mainly used as desserts are considered fruits. Actually cooked vegetables constitute our principal meals while fruits are consumed as desserts. Thus cucumber and tomato are botanically fruits but they are mainly vegetables.

Fruits and vegetables — their importance

It is an accepted and well-settled fact that cooking or heat destroys nutritive value of the vegetables. The tender leaves and stems of fresh vegetables contain the highest percentage of vitamins and minerals. If they are consumed fresh in a raw state (as expressed juice), it will be highly beneficial for the body to keep fit and healthy.

Many elements are required to make a diet that is nutritionally adequate and no single natural food can supply all. Vegetables supply some elements in which other food materials are deficient and they neutralise acid substances produced in the course of digestion of meats, cheese and ghee-prepared foods. The dark green leafy vegetables are rich source of carotene which is converted by the body into vitamin A. Vitamin C is also amply provided by leafy and green vegetables.

Few vegetables are valuable sources of proteins or carbohydrates; beans and peas are rich in iron and proteins; potatoes and sweet potatoes are important sources of carbohydrates; citrous fruits supply most of the vitamins including ascorbic acid in plenty.

For this reason there is now a growing tendency to consume more vegetables and fruits in their raw states.

Vegetables that are usually consumed in their raw state

All vegetables can't be consumed in their raw state. Some important vegetables are isolated by the medical scientists for healing purposes. They are carrots, beans, spinach, parsley, turnip, watercress, cucumber, tomato, garlic, onion, fennel, string beans, Brussels sprouts, lady's finger, lemon, celery, lettuce, radish, papaya, green jack-fruit, cabbage etc.

Classification of fruits

The structure and the origin of different fruits are extremely varied, but there are also similarities so that various types of fruits can be classified. A simple fruit is the product of a single pistil while a compound fruit is derived from two or more pistils. Both simple and compound fruits may be partly derived from other parts of the flower or from the flower stalk in addition to the pistils. Such fruits are called accessory fruit. The raspberry and pineapple are compound accessory fruits. Simple fruits may be fleshy or dry.

Simple fleshy fruits

One of the major types of simple fleshy fruits is the berry. The term 'berry' is applied to pulpy fruits like tomatoes, grapes, blue-berries. Leathery skinned fleshy fruits are oranges, limes, kumquats, grape fruits etc. Hard skinned fleshy fruits are cucumbers and melons.

The second major type of fleshy fruit is the drupe or stone-fruit like cherry, peach and olive. The pome is fleshy accessory fruit such as the apple or pear.

Simple dry fruits

Simple dry fruits are dehiscent or indehiscent. Dehiscent fruits open when matured to release the seeds. Indehiscent fruits remain closed throughout the period of their development. Dehiscent fruits are pea and bean. Indehiscent fruits are butter-cup and buck wheat.

Compound fruits

There are two general types of compound fruits, viz. aggregate and multiple fruits, each of which is the product of two or more pistils in one flower. They are straw-berries, rasp-berries and black-berries.

Multiple fruits

They sometimes look superficially like aggregate fruits but these are products of many separate flowers that unite into a fleshy, closely packed mass as they mature. The mulberry, pineapple, breadfruit and the orange are good examples of multiple fruits.

Classification of vegetables

Vegetables are classified on the basis of the part of the plant such as root, stem or tuber that is used for food.

Root vegetables:- The root group includes beets, carrots, radishes, rutabagas, turnips and yams.

Stem vegetables:- The stem group includes asparagus and kohlarabi.

Tuber vegetables:- The tuber is an underground stem. Edible tubers include girasole or Jerusalem artichoke, potato, taro, and yam.

Leaf and leaf-stalk vegetables:- The leaf group includes Brussels sprouts, cabbage, celery, chard, chicory, endive, lettuce, parsley, rhubarb (pie) and spinach.

Bulb vegetables:- The bulb group includes garlic, leek, and onion.

Immature inflorescence vegetables:- This group includes artichokes, broccoli and cauliflower.

Fruits used as vegetables:- The immature fruits are used as vegetables, viz. cow-pea, cucumber, papaya, jack-fruit (ichar), egg-plant (brinjal), Lima bean, okra, pea, summer squash (gourd).

Mature fruit vegetables:- This group includes musk-melon, pumpkin, tomato and water-melon.

Dr. S. Davidson has said, 'Vegetables and fruits all have nutritive properties. Although 70% or more of their weight is water, still they contain vitamin C and carotene, the two nutrients which cereals lack. Fresh fruits particularly of the citrus variety and their juices are usually rich in vitamin C but vegetables are an uncertain source as this vitamin C is easily destroyed by cooking or heat. Vegetables contain indigestible cellular matters which adds bulk to the intestinal content and is useful in preventing constipation. Vegetables also provide calcium and iron but they are destroyed by cooking. Vegetables and fruits taken in their raw state will certainly provide maximum nutrient to the body.'

Dr. M. Pyke has said, 'Food is anything taken into the body which is capable of supplying physical energy, promoting growth, repairing tissue and furnishing energy for bodily heat and work and aid in protection from diseases. Man is the only animal who does not know instinctively how to select his right food and so the science of dietetics has developed. He is also the only animal who cooks his food which may become less digestible and not so nutritious as they are in their natural raw state. On the other hand heat destroys natural vitamins and minerals to a great extent. The green leafy and yellow vegetables like spinach, carrots, beet, garlic, onion etc. taken in their raw state will certainly provide natural vitamins in plenty.

Dr. Lloyd E. Lewis has said, 'The green leafy and yellow vegetables like spinach, kale, carrots and sweet potatoes contribute vitamin A, riboflavin and iron to the diet if taken raw. The citrus fruits, tomato and raw cabbage furnish ascorbic acid, iron while other vegetables and fruits may provide other vitamins and minerals. Therefore the major sources of chief vitamins, calcium and iron are the green, leafy and yellow vegetables. They should be consumed in their raw state as far as practicable.'

Dr. Benedict Lust has said, 'It is deplorable that a large part of the nutritive value of our foods is lost by irrational preparation, particularly over-cooking. The tender leaves and stems of fresh vegetables contain the largest percentage of alkaline bases; hence they are not only useful as garnishes but should feature as salads, juices and vegetable dishes.'

Dr. Eva Hill, a cancer specialist of the Auckland General Hospital, New York, has said, 'Man is the sickest animal on earth and he is the only one that mucks about with food. Eat your food the way God made it. Cancer is only one of the degenerative diseases increasingly afflicting those who eat and drink unnatural foods dosed with pesticides and reared on or grown on depleted soils.'

Chief causes of diseases and their remedies

Diseases are mainly caused due to two reasons, excessive heat in the body and excessive cold in the body. If there is excessive heat in the body, it causes boils, abscesses, headache, vomiting, high blood pressure, heart-attack, stroke, allergic ailments, diarrhoea etc. You can get instant relief from these ailments if you drink juice of cold producing fruits or vegetables like cucumber, lime (musumbi), lemon, papaya, marmelos, garlic, onion, tomato, banana etc.

If there is excessive cold in the body, especially during the rainy season or during winter months, it may develop diseases like toothache, gumache, earache, mumps, high fevers, coughs and colds, bronchitis, asthma, low blood pressure, low vitality, lassitude, general debility, weakness etc. You can get instant relief if you drink juice of heat producing fruits and vegetables like orange (narangi), carrot, beet, cashew nut, hickory nut, ground-nut, peas, gram etc. During hot summer months, you should try to drink juices of cold producing fruits in plenty. Please remember this point very carefully.

It is said that germs do not cause any disease but they appear in the same way as flies do when garbage is lying about. If there is no filth or garbage, there will be no flies; no germs and no disease. As our body is filled with waste products and they are not cleared properly, diseases invade the body. This is the root cause of all diseases.

The best way to clear the body of its waste products is to drink raw fruit juices in adequate quantities. All fruits do not have the quality or power of removing waste products from the body most effectively. There are two miraculous fruits which can do this job properly. These two fruits are LIME

(Musumbi or Sarbati lebu) and PINEAPPLE (Anaras). If you take a glass of musumbi juice (lime) in the morning, your bowels will be cleared nicely and you will remain free from all sorts of diseases. This is the secret of maintaining perfect health. If your health remains good, you can work more, earn more, enjoy more. What more do you want?

It is said, 'Toxicity is the primary and root cause of all diseases. Toxicity is the only sickness that exists in the human body.' Detoxification of the whole body is absolutely necessary in order to escape from the attack of degenerative diseases. Proper detoxification of the whole body can be done most effectively by consuming raw fresh fruit juices. No other food can give such perfect detoxification of the whole body. Now the key to prevention of all sorts of degenerative diseases like cancer, arthritis, diabetes and heart-attack is 'detoxification'. This means that you should take a glass of raw musumbi or sarbati lebu juice once a week in order to clear off the whole body of its waste products. This is the only way to keep yourself fit and active.

It has been found that persons who live only on natural foods, i.e. raw fruits and vegetables, thrive best or live longer without any ailment in the body as in the case of our ancient saints and sages who used to live up to 100 years and only on raw fruits and vegetables. On the other hand, persons who live only on cooked foods get frequent attacks of bodily ailments.

Cooking destroys the natural vitamins and minerals. Vitamin C is a labile substance which is easily destroyed by heat and chemicals. In raw fruits and vegetables you will get all vitamins intact.

Dr. Harry Benjamin has said, 'Cooking destroys normal vitamins present in the fruits and vegetables. It would be better if we take raw fruit and vegetable juices in order to keep our body fit, healthy and active. It will surely help us to live longer'.

Eat your food the way God made it

Over 2400 years ago, Hippocrates, the father of medicine, said, 'Let living (natural) food be thy medicine'. In these simple words, he tried to explain that in raw fruits and vegetables lie the essential drug to control and fight human ailments most effectively. Through modern conception of this ancient idea, many body upsets, acute and chronic, have been miraculously corrected. It has been proved that proper nutrition in the natural way is the key to our survival.

Dr. Ann Wigmore in her book 'Be your own doctor' has said, 'Wild animals in their natural environment are rarely found sick. Yet domesticated animals, cared for and fed by men are seldom found well. Wild animals select their food through instinct alone and make few mistakes. Domesticated animals must eat what human beings feed them and consequently they suffer from a multitude of diseases'.

Dr. G. P. Erap-Thomas, author of 'Organic soil' found on research that when cooked food was eaten, it permitted tumours and cancerous growths to build within the body. But when substituted with living food (raw fruits and vegetables) these tumours and cancerous growths immediately began to shrink for lack of nourishment.

Dr. Ann Wigmore in her book 'Why suffer' has said, 'The heat of cooking is not the only way to kill food enzymes and nutrients. Excess acidity in the stomach also destroys their effectiveness. The easiest way to add living enzymes of the right type to the digestive tract is to eat ripe fruit, uncooked organically grown vegetables, sprouts and wheatgrass. We need to turn to living foods, uncooked foods that have the ability to strengthen our bodies through their electrical impulses, enzymes and nutrients. Cooked and processed food does not provide the complex structure of the protein molecules and destroys the associated enzymes necessary for their utilisation, rendering them less useful.'

So for the human body, uncooked food is the only of nutrition required for its survival. Cooked food is considered as dead and actually unsuitable and unsafe for the human body. He should try to avoid cooked food as far as practicable.

Drugs and operative methods on the body come and go. But fruit juice therapy has survived and flourished through the ages because of its unique benefits. Fruit juice therapy is very strong and effective as it removes the defect from the root. It has got no side-effects or after-effects. It does not damage any part of the body as drugs do. It does not form any habit. These are not narcotics. So fruit juice does not cause any damage to the nerves as most drugs do. It does not cause any adverse reactions either physically or mentally. Over and above fruits and vegetables are rather cheap in comparison with costly drugs. So it will reduce your medical expenses.

Nature has provided us with some life-saving fruits like musumbi, orange, garlic, onion, margosa, marmelos, papaya, cucumber, bitter-gourd etc. Nature is still regarded as the most welcome healer.

In old age, you can't keep your body healthy by taking drugs. But if you take fried garlics, and musumbi juice, you will be perfectly all right. This is the secret of keeping long life.

Dr. Eva Hill, a cancer specialist, has said, 'Eat your food the way God has made it, i.e. in their raw state. Cancer is caused only due to the consumption of irrational, cooked or dead foods. Cancer is nothing but a vitamin deficiency disease.' She herself was a cancer patient. She had cancer in her face but she became completely cured by taking only raw fruits and vegetables for some time.

Dr. John B. Lust in his book 'Raw Juice Therapy' has said, 'Natural healing is the most desirable factor for the survival of the human race. It is a return to nature in methods of living and treatment. It makes use of the elementary forces of nature, of chemical selection of foods that will constitute a correct medical dietary. There is really but one healing force in existence and that is Nature herself; that is the inherent restorative power of the organisms to overcome diseases.'

Dr. John Barret in his book 'Cancer and cure' has said, ' What we eat nowadays is largely poisoned, adulterated food, forced by unnatural methods to grow on depleted soil and further poisoned by insect sprays, the traces of which can never be completely removed from the fruits and vegetables we buy; we cannot detoxify the body without taking raw fruit and vegetable juices.'

Dr. Harry Hoxsey in his book 'You don't have to die' has said, 'An imbalance in the body chemistry and cell metabolism is one of the key factors in the development of cancer.' His treatment consisted chiefly in removing this inbalance of body chemistry and cell metabolism by consuming raw fruit and vegetable juices. He cured skin cancer patients by simply fixing one crushed garlic on the affected part with a sticking plaster and kept the patient under raw fruit juice therapy for some time. He observed that cancerous cells disappeared like magic in a very short time. His theory ushered in a new era and new hope to suffering mankind in general.

Overconsumption or obesity

By far the commonest effect of continued overconsumption of calories is obesity — a state of excess accumulation of fat in the body.

Obesity is becoming more and more a problem in developed countries and among privileged communities. In simplest terms, it is caused by persistent consumption of more calories than are required to meet the energy expenditure of that particular person. Endocrine changes at puberty, during pregnancy and at the menopause may contribute to obesity at these stages of life. Some say that some defect in nervous control may lead to abnormal deposition of fat in certain fat depots.

Obese persons have reduced life expectancy and their life insurance premiums are generally high. They suffer from a number of diseases and disabilities. The tendency toward obesity and susceptibility to these diseases both may be inherited. Diabetes of the middle-aged is strongly associated with obesity and there is association of obesity in females with gallbladder disease. Coronary heart disease and obesity are closely related. Obesity is a mechanical load on the lower spine and the major weight bearing joints — hips, knees and ankles. Reduction of weight may mitigate the middle-age tendency to degenerative diseases of the joints and rheumatism. Obesity of the trunk may interfere with breathing and may contribute to pulmonary heart disease. Obesity is associated with proneness to accident. Obese men are generally impotent.

Drug is not the restorer of good health but means of further disease

Drugs usually cause temporary relief from disease. They also cause serious side-effects or after-effects in the body. Supposed pain-killers like aspirin, novalgin, analgin, anacin, crocin etc. may give you temporary relief from pain or headache or bodyache but they do cause permanent damage to the heart, liver and kidneys. A more serious trouble is likely to develop later. This is a serious drawback.

Narcotic drugs like morphine, atropine, codeine etc. cause serious damage to the nervous system. Constant consumption of sedatives, anodynes or pain-killers may paralyse your nerve action and may cause mental derangement. Sleeping pills are very dangerous. Constant use of such pills may damage the entire nervous system permanently. Constant consumption of antibiotic drugs may cause skin eruptions, black and white patches in the entire body skin. Nowadays many people have been found to be suffering from this type of black and white patches which has turned into a permanent disability. This is due to overconsumption of antibiotic drugs.

So drug is not the way to good health but it is the way to further disease. Raw fruit juices have been found on research by medical men to be the best and the most safe method to fight dreadful diseases. Again it is the most surest way to overcome any sort of ailment in the body.

Cooked food is dangerous

Medical men have found after research that the only sickness in the human body is TOXICITY. Toxicity is the root cause of all diseases. Anyhow the whole body is required to be detoxified in order to keep away all sorts of diseases. So detoxification is the synonym for good health.

Imbalance in the body chemistry and cell metabolism causes all sorts of degenerative diseases like cancer, arthritis, diabetes, and heart attack. This imbalance is caused by constant consumption of irrational (cooked) foods.

It has been found that persons who live only on natural foods, i.e. raw fruits, and vegetables, thrive best or live longer without any ailment in the body, like ancient saints and sages who lived for 100 years only on raw fruits and vegetables. On the other hand, persons who live only on cooked foods get frequent attacks of bodily ailments. Why?

The main reason is that cooking destroys the natural vitamins and minerals. Vitamin C is a labile substance which is easily destroyed by heat and chemicals. In raw fruits and vegetables, you will get all vitamins intact. One special benefit is that it heals a particular disease from its root.

Chlorophyll

Blackiston's Gould Medical Dictionary defines chlorophyll as under:

'It is the green colouring matter responsible for photosynthesis in plants. It consists of Chlorophyll-A and Chlorophyll-B. It is used as a colouring agent and medically in the treatment of lesions and as deodorant.'

Chlorophyll in plant leaves would cure many bodily ailments including degenerative diseases like cancer, diabetes, jaundice, arthritis and heart-attack.

Dr. Ann Wigmore in her book 'Be your own doctor' has said, 'One simple remedy for helping people is the God given chlorophyll of the wheatgrass. Nature uses it as a body cleanser, rebuilder and neutraliser of toxins.'

Chlorophyll found in the leaves of certain vegetables like spinach, Brussels sprouts, cabbage, beet-root, carrot, garlic, onion, lemon etc. are very useful in curing various sorts of bodily ailments completely. It has been found that vitamin U deficiency causes gastric ulcer, and if raw cabbage juice is given to gastric ulcer patients they respond to it very quickly.

Dr. S. Firenczi, a cancer specialist of Hungary, cured in 1950 many tumour patients by raw beet juice (1 kg daily). He found remarkable results in 15 out of 16 cases; the cancerous growths were definitely reduced; the patients gained 6 to 21 pounds and their blood count changed for the better. He found very remarkable results in curing many cancer patients only through raw red beet juice therapy.

Dr. John B. Lust of the United States treated and cured many colitis patients with raw fruit juice. Colitis is a disturbance of the intestinal tract characterised by inflammation of the large intestine. It is frequently of nervous origin and constipation is usually a strong factor. He cured many colitis patients with lime, lemon, garlic, orange and carrot juices.

Dr. Richard Willstate has observed that the chlorophyll molecule bears close resemblance to haemoglobin, the red pigment in the human blood, and differs only in the central element which in blood is iron and in chlorophyll magnesium. So it is the natural blood building element of the human being.

Dr. Bircher, a medical scientist, has called chlorophyll as 'concentrated sun-power'. He has said that chlorophyll increases the function of the heart, effects vascular system, intestine, uterus and lungs. It is a great tonic which keeps human body healthy and strong.

The juices of fresh fruits and vegetables play a vital role in restoring and maintaining optimum health. Tennyson once musing with a tiny flower realised that if he could find out the secret of its minute existence, he would understand the meaning and greatness of life. What Tennyson had said of the flower is equally true of living fresh fruits and vegetables. Locked within their millions of cells are not only vitamins, minerals, enzymes and nutrients but life itself. Raw fruits and vegetables actually play a very vital role in keeping our body fit and active.

Fruit juice can be taken at any hour during the day or night. For quickening energy, relieving fatigue and bolstering up low spirits nothing surpasses them. They are life-giving, youth giving and health giving vital foods.

Dr. Paul Bragg has said, 'The continuous and persistent practice of getting the liquid life of fruits and vegetables into the system is one of the secrets of keeping young. They revitalize the blood stream, giving a sparkle to the eye, colour to the lips and a spring to the step'.

Dr. Mercy C. Hogle has said, 'The most gratifying revelation is that people stricken with serious disorders like cancer, arthritis, heart-attack could, by taking enough of it, become strong, active, robust and fully cured'.

Dr. John B. Lust has said, 'Fresh fruit juices are the cleansers of the human system. Vegetable juices are regeneratives and builders of the body. Grown in healthy soil, they contain all the substances needed for nourishing the human body, provided the juices are used fresh, raw and without preservatives'.

Medical men tell us that many diseases are the results of a diet deficient in trace vitamins and organic materials. Such diseases are pellagra, beriberi, rickets, scurvy, malnutrition, anaemia, obesity, common cold etc. Fresh fruit and vegetable juices satisfy and nourish our body most effectively. They revitalise the blood-stream. They revivify the nerves. They rejuvenate the glands and organs. They soothe the acid irritated nerves.

Dr. Henry Lindlahr has said, 'The greatest achievement of nature cure philosophy lies in the fact that it has reduced the treatment of acute and subacute diseases, as well as of chronic ailments to the greatest simplicity'.

'The secret of longevity largely lies in eating intelligently. Learn to like foods that are food for you'. — Dr. Gayelord Hauser.

'It is deplorable that a large part of the nutritive value of our foods is lost by irrational preparation, particularly by overcooking. The tender leaves and stems of fresh vegetables contain the largest percentage of alkaline bases; hence they are not only useful as garnishes but should be featured as salads, juices and vegetable dishes'.—Dr. John B. Lust.

THE FRUITS AND VEGETABLES

'The great dietetic and hygienic value of pure fruit juices is not yet appreciated by the vast majority of people. Fruits differ from practically all other foods by the fact that their nutritive elements exist in the soluble forms of organic sugar, dextrin, and fruit acids which are found almost exclusively in their juices. The dry pulp left after the extraction of the juice contains almost nothing except cellulose and little protein. It is therefore inaccurate to deny that pure fruit juices of all sorts are exceedingly wholesome for they contain all the valuable properties of the fruits from which they are extracted.' — Dr. John B. Lust.

'The almost immediate effects experienced by a fatigued person after taking pure fruit juice is due to the nutritious energy released by its fruit sugar content almost instantaneously utilized by the body. Natural fruit sugar is a great source of potential energy.' — Dr. Gayelord Hauser.

1. Garlic (Rashun or lahsan):

Botanically it is known as Allium sativum. It is a bulbous perennial plant of the lily family (Liliaceae) used to flavour foods. The aroma is powerful and onion-like, the taste is pungent. A classic ingredient in many national cuisines, garlic has become popular in the United States since World War II. In ancient and medieval times garlic was used as a medicine. The bulb contains antibiotic allium and it has antiseptic properties and is an expectorant and intestinal antispasmodic. Fresh garlic is used to flavour meats, stews, sauces and salads. Garlic powder made from ground dehydrated bulbs is often used in cooking as a substitute for fresh garlic. It is also used by the meat-packing industry in prepared meats. Garlic salt, a mixture of garlic powder and table salt, is another seasoning for cooking.

Garlic has been used since ancient times in the treatment of various diseases. Crushed garlic is sometimes applied to the skin to alleviate the pain of insect bites or scorpion stings. Popular belief has credited garlic with the ability to ward off disease and evil spirits.

Virgil and Pliny both wrote in praise of its medicinal virtues. It is probably one of the most powerful antiseptics known to man; catarrh simply cannot persist against garlic. Its oil penetrates to almost every single tissue of the body and can actually be treated within hours after eating just one or two cloves. All kinds of worms are destroyed by garlic. The dose varies from one to three cloves of garlic eaten raw and preferably chewed slowly.

Garlic contains vitamin A, B, C and D in plenty. Some doctors found that garlic contained calcium, iron, phosphorus, iodine, acrolein (which kills germs), crotonic aldehyde, allyl sulphide and volatile terpenes.

Hippocrates, the father of medicine, has said, 'If one chews a clove of garlic everyday and swallows its juice, one will remain free from all sorts of diseases.' Such is the great power of medicinal properties of garlic.

Garlic was highly honoured in ancient Egypt and thousands of slaves working on the great Pyramid were fed garlic daily in order to keep them free from diseases. In ancient times, the soldiers relied on garlic to give them added strength in battle. The phoenicians and vikings carried large amounts of garlic with them on their sea voyages. In Bulgaria, there was a surprising number of people who reached the age of

100 years and were still active and working. In that country, it was a common practice to chew garlic regularly. The Chinese, Greeks, Romans, Hindus, Egyptians and Babylonians all claimed that garlic cured intestinal and lung disorders, flatulence, constipation, worms, infections of the respiratory system, skin diseases, wounds and aging. Aristophanes regarded the juice as a restorer of masculine vigour. Pliny stated that garlic had very powerful medicinal properties and added that even its odour drove away serpents and scorpions. During the middle ages, when the horrible plague ravaged Europe, it was said that those who ate garlic daily were not infected.

Dr. John Gunn in his book 'The home book of health' has described garlic as a stimulant, diuretic and expectorant and if applied to the skin, rubefacient that it is, it will produce a blister. The medicinal uses of garlic are numerous. It is being recommended by some doctors as a valuable expectorant in consumption and all affections of the lungs; by some others as an important diuretic in dropsy and as a remedy for worms and is often given to children for that purpose. It is an excellent remedy in nervous and spasmodic coughs, hoarseness and the like and may be given in the form of a syrup, tinctures or in substances but the best way to use it is to express the juice and mix it either with syrup or some other vehicles like honey.

Richard Lucas has described in the book 'Nature's Medicines' garlic as very useful in asthma, cough and cold, bronchitis, intestinal disorders, constipation, high blood pressure and urinary troubles. It keeps one young. Evidences have proved that garlic is a blood pressure regulator. It also cures indigestion, disinfects the bowels, kills putrefying bacteria in the large intestines; neutralises poisons in the organism itself. If one puts a piece of garlic in his mouth at the onset of cold, the cold will disappear within a few hours or a day.

Garlic has a curative effect on chronic diseases in the upper respiratory organs provided one keeps a garlic in his mouth day and night renewing the cloves. This is also applied to clinical infection of the tonsils, salivary glands and neighbouring lymph glands, severe pharyngitis, laryngitis and bronchitis.

Garlic makes loose teeth take root again, removes tartar and has a curative effect on eye catarrh and inflammation of the lacrymal duct as well as of the middle-ear. Pimples disappear without leaving a scar if rubbed several times daily with garlic juice but this does not prevent the formation of new pimples. Purification of the skin must take place through the blood. During World War II, the Russians discovered that garlic placed on unclean wounds of soldiers cleaned these wounds in four or five days. Grated garlic placed near the most vicious bacteria will kill them in five minutes.

In Germany, Fusagauger and Bechar found in 1931 that garlic was an effective remedy in intestinal and lung disorders. French scientist Poullard found that garlic caused a decided drop in blood pressure. Amano and Kitagower of Japan reported in 1935 that garlic possessed antiseptic properties which were effective against typhoid bacillus.

Jewish scientist Dr. Albert Schwaitzer employed garlic in typhoid and cholera and obtained miraculous results. He confirmed that garlic certainly possessed miraculous healing powers. In Russia, garlic was commonly known as 'Russian Penicillin'. Almost all Russians eat garlic daily and their average longevity rose beyond 100 years of age.

J.F. Dastur has said in his book 'Medicinal plants of India and Pakistan' that garlic resembles squill in its medicinal properties; it is given in fevers, coughs, flatulence, disorders of the nervous system, agues, dropsical affections, pulmonary phthisis, whooping cough, gangrene of the lung and dilated bronchi. Garlic in the form of syrup is a valuable remedy for asthma, hoarseness and disorders of the chest and lungs. Externally garlic is used as rubefacient, vesicant and disinfectant. It is applied on indolent tumours, ulcerated surfaces and wounds; a poultice of the bulb is used for scrofulous sores and ringworm. A clove of garlic is introduced in the ear passage for relief of earache. As a rubefacient, garlic is locally used in sciatica, paralysis and neuralgic pains. The oil extracted from the seeds is given for checking cold, fits of intermittent fevers. As a liniment, it is used for paralytic and rheumatic affections.

Dr. M. Kraig has said in his book 'Green Medicines' that garlic is the best individual treatment found to get rid of tubercle bacillus, no matter what part of the body is affected, whether skin, bones, glands, lungs or private parts. Thus nature has given us specific treatment of tuberculosis by diet, rest, exercise, sun-baths and garlic.

He has also confirmed that garlic is a sure remedy for all sorts of intestinal disorders. Daily use of garlic cures stomach troubles, lung troubles, dysentery, diarrhoea and heart palpitations. All symptoms will certainly vanish if garlic is taken continuously for six weeks.

Dr. Swinburn Clymer, in his book 'The Medicines of Nature', has expressed the view that garlic juice causes a decided drop in blood pressure and checks sudden attack of stroke. He was of the view that one should take or chew garlic day and night renewing the cloves that have absorbed poisons till full recovery is obtained.

Ayurvedacharya Sivakali Bhattacharjee in his book 'Chiranjib Banausadhi' has highly praised the medicinal virtues of garlic. According to him, garlic juice applied externally on septic boils, abscess, carbuncles, tumours, insect bites, dogbites, scorpion stings etc. cures these ailments miraculously. Garlic chewed raw every morning cures cough and cold, elephantiasis, gall-stones, high blood pressure, nervous disorders, diphtheria, skin eruptions, worms, whooping cough, tuberculosis and heart troubles.

A.W. Hatfield has described in his book 'Pleasure of Herbs' the medicinal virtues of garlic which were recognised since time immemorial. Pliny gave an exceedingly long list of its curative uses and Gallen praised it as 'Heal-all'. Chaucer and old writers referred to it as 'Poor man's treacle'. Shakespeare also praised the medicinal virtues of garlic in 'A midsummer night's dream' and also in 'Measure for Measure'. In ancient Greece, no one not having eaten garlic was allowed to enter the temple of Cybele.

Sir R.N. Chopra has mentioned in his book 'Indigenous drugs of India' that garlic juice is most powerful remedy for cough and cold, bronchitis, tuberculosis, stomach disorders and urinary troubles.

K.R. Kirtikar in his book 'Indian Medicinal Plants' has expressed the view that garlic is a sure remedy for cough and cold, bronchitis, heart troubles, tuberculosis, high blood pressure, intestinal troubles, urinary disorders and kidney ailments.

2. Lemon (Lebu/nimbu):

Botanically it is called Citrus acid. It is a small tree or spreading bush of the rue family (Rutaceae). The lemon forms a spreading bush or a small tree 10 to 20 feet high if not trained or pruned. Its young leaves have a decidedly reddish tint; later they turn green. In some varieties, the young leaves of the lemon are angular; some have sharp thorns at the axilae of the leaves. The flowers having a sweet odour are rather large, solitary or in small clusters in the axilae of the leaves. Reddish tinted in the bud, the petals are white above and reddish purple below.

The fruit is oval with a broad low apical nipple and having 8 to 10 segments. The outer rind or peel is yellow when ripe and rather thick in some varieties is prominently glandular dotted. The white spongy inner part of the peel called the mesocarp is nearly tasteless and is the chief source of commercial grades of pectin. The seeds are small, ovoid, pointed, sometimes few or more. The pulp is decidedly acid. Young lemon starts bearing fruits as early as the third year after planting and commercial crop may be expected during the fifth year. The average orchard yield per tree is 1500 lemons a year.

The humble lemon contains most of the vitamins and minerals. It has magical and wonderful healing powers. It is a citrus fruit. Other citrus fruits are orange, mandarine, tangerine, narangi, musumbi (lime), grape-fruit, grape, and shaddock. All citrus fruits are very rich sources of vitamins A, B and C. They also contain appreciable amounts of iron and calcium.

Vitamin C:

Vitamin C in the diet helps the body to grow and maintain collagen. They explain that collagen is a gelatin-like gristle that holds billions of cells together in the body. It is found in ligaments, joints, bones, gum tissues and in the walls of all the blood vessels.

It also gives elasticity and strength to the connective tissue. Again vitamin C is necessary to the normal healing rate of wounds and to prevent bruises from discolouring the skin for too long time. Its function is also to strengthen the body's resistance to infection and maintain tissue integrity of teeth, bones and gums.

Vitamin C in adequate quantity must be taken daily and if its deficiency is continued over a long period of time, the gums may become tender and bleed easily, joints may hurt and swell, black and blue marks may appear readily at the slightest bruise, the chance of haemorrhage which may result from a 'stroke' is far greater and colds may be taken frequently. Deficiency of vitamin C may cause scurvy. Therefore vitamin C is absolutely necessary to fortify the body against infections and cold.

Daily requirement of vitamin C:

Men	- 75 mg
Women	- 70 mg
Lactating women	- 150 mg
Pregnant women	- 100 mg
Infants	- 30 mg

Children :
    1 to 3 yrs. - 35 mg
    4 to 6 yrs. - 50 mg
    7 to 9 yrs. - 60 mg

Boys :

10 to 12 yrs.	- 75 mg
13 to 15 yrs.	- 80 mg
16 to 20 yrs.	- 100 mg

Girls :

10 to 12 yrs.	- 75 mg
13 to 15 yrs.	- 80 mg
16 to 20 yrs.	- 80 mg

Fruits containing vitamin C

Whole orange	- 75 mg
4 oz orange juice	- 50 mg
Large grape fruit	- 150 mg
Medium size tangerine	- 25 mg
Lemon juice 1 tablespoonful	- 7 mg
Lime (musumbi)	- 75 mg

Where extra vitamin C is needed

1. **Smoking and alcoholic beverages:** It is found on research that smoking causes great damage to vitamin C content in the human body. One cigarette destroys 25 mg of vitamin C in the body which means that 500 mg is neutralised for every packet of cigarettes smoked. If smoking is continued throughout the morning, the store of

vitamin C will be entirely neutralised. To replace, foods containing vitamin C (ascorbic acid) must be taken during lunch, although this replacement will also be depleted if one continues to smoke in the afternoon. So a habitual smoker will always require much more vitamin C than the non-smoker. This will explain why those who smoke are more prone to infections than those who do not.

2. **Stress, strain and fatigue:** Stress disorders demand increased intake of vitamin C. It is found that some fifty common disorders are attributed to stress and strain.

3. **Diseases and injuries:** Patients suffering from burns or injuries require increased intake of vitamin C which is necessary for tissue regeneration. The use of antibiotics or barbiturates also causes deficiency of vitamin C in the body. So citrus fruits must be consumed in adequate quantities daily in order to keep healthy.

4. **Old age (aging):** Older people require more vitamin C than younger people. It is found that large quantities of vitamin C strengthen the capillaries in certain vascular diseases like diabetes. Citrus fruits as a source of vitamin C and other nutrients are a particularly important food for persons whose normal digestive functions have been disturbed by illness or advanced age. The high vitamin C content of citrus fruits will not only tend to restore normalcy but also

it will militate against further infection and help to heal tissue and capillary lesions.

A senile person is forgetful, confused and his speech rambles. He repeats a question that has been just answered. Memory is so poor that the individual does not recognise members of his own family. So senile patients and those approaching old age need substantial quantities of vitamin C to protect their brain from damage and to fight infections.

Ascorbic acid alone may be used in the preservation of vitamin C and treatment for deficiency, but the natural juices of citrus fruits will be more efficient and more complete in their action. In the citrus fruits, ascorbic acid is always accompanied by a bonus of other vital nutrients which nature in her wisdom has supplied. But the citrus fruits or juices should be taken fresh.

Nutritional value of citrus fruits: Citrus fruits are rich in vitamin C and also contain numerous other vitamin factors, especially A, inositol and certain of vitamin B complex. They also supply appreciable supplementary amounts of minerals with which it becomes easy to maintain health properly. Minerals build rich blood, strong bones, nerve tissues and assist in regulating the body. Calcium found in orange makes them a valuable food for infants as it is necessary for growing bodies. Oranges are likewise useful for older people.

Lemons as medicine: Lemon juice cures menorrhagia, nose-bleeding, hepatitis, gastric ulcer if taken several times daily. Of all foods which have also been used as medicines, lemons are the most commonly known. The custom of using a slice of lemon when eating a fish dinner was originally intended for remedial purposes rather than for flavouring. It was believed that if a fish bone were to be accidentally swallowed during the meal, the juice of lemon could dissolve it. Lemons have been used as a household remedy for colds, rheumatism, sore throat, gastric and liver troubles, headache, heartburn, biliousness etc. Lemon juice mixed with glycerine is used for chapped lips or chilblains. For constipation, the juice of a lemon is taken in a glass of hot water one-half hour before breakfast. Local application of lemon juice is used to allay irritation caused by bites of gnats and similar insects.

Dr. Fred R. Klenner has described most elaborately the various uses of lemon in his book 'The Key to Good Health : Vitamin C'. He has said that lemon juice is very useful in arthritis, cold, hypertension, sun-stroke and menorrhagia.

Lemon juice in diseases

1. **Arthritis, rheumatic diseases:** A few drinks of lemon juice is the surest remedy for rheumatic fever, painful joints, lumbago and sciatica. There will be no cardiac complications. Those with incipient arthritis were given ascorbic acid therapy and similar results were achieved.

2. **Common cold:** Lemon juice or vitamin C tablets taken three or four times daily along with garlic cures cough and cold.

3. **Oedema:** Oedema of the muscular region produced by vascular decompensation often responds more rapidly when 10 to 33 ounces of orange or grape-fruit juice is given in addition to 500 mg of vitamin C for three or four days.

4. **Hypertension, and cardiovascular diseases in the aged:** Many illnesses of the aged may be prevented with an adequate intake of vitamin C daily. Particularly cerebrovascular diseases and heart disorders may be largely reduced.

5. **Prickly heat:** Quick relief is obtained by taking a few drinks of lemon juice daily.

6. **Shock:** To prevent surgical shock surgeons apply ascorbic acid routinely before and after surgery. 500 mg by mouth one hour before surgery to patients of average weight helps to combat traumatic shock. Vitamin C is extremely useful in preventing shock and post-operative weakness.

7. **Menorrhagia and haemorrhage:** A few drinks of lemon juice or narangi juice will certainly give some relief in acute menorrhagia.

8. **Asthma:** Many cases of asthma have been relieved by taking a half-spoonful of lemon-juice before each meal and upon retiring.

9. **Cough and cold:** Roasted lemon when properly prepared is on e of the most effective remedies for cough and cold.

10. **Corns:** Lemon juice applied to corns a few times a day makes an effective remedy. Bind the corn and leave it overnight, you can expect wonderful results.

11. **Headache:** Lemon tea relieves headache.

12. **Heartburn:** If you take one glass of lemon juice, you will surely get relief from it.

13. **Nausea, vomiting and travel sickness:** If one takes a glass of lemon juice before leaving home, one can return from travelling without any trouble.

14. **Sun-stroke or heat-stroke:** Lemon or lime (musumbi) juice prevents sun-stroke or heat-stroke.

15. **Whooping cough:** Lemon or musumbi (lime) juice is a household remedy for whooping cough.

16. **Weakness and general debility:** Lemon or musumbi (lime) juice offers an excellent remedy in general debility and weakness.

17. **Low vitality:** Lemon or lime (musumbi) juice removes this condition very quickly.

Other uses: removing stains: Use clear lemon juice; it will remove stains from the hands.

Dr. Fred R. Klenner in his book 'The Key to Good Health: Vitamin C' has also confirmed the above-mentioned uses of lemon.

Dr. Donald Law in his book 'Herbs for cooking and for healing' has said that there are over 20 varieties of lemon but the juice of all of them is most helpful as a remedy for purifying the blood, for rubbing into the scalp against falling hair. Lemon juice mixed with shampoo acts as a tonic to the scalp. From medieval times the skin of lemon has been chewed to act as a cleaner of teeth and strengthener of gums. Naturopaths frequently recommend a course of lemon juice and water to rid the body of accumulated poisons and debris. You can extract more juice from a lemon if you place it in an oven for a few minutes and bake it slowly. The humble lemon contains vitamin A, B, C, G and the rare vitamin P.

Lemon juice cures erysipelas, carbuncle and abscess. Dysentery quickly disappears after a few drinks of pure lemon or musumbi juice. Some naturopaths also cured diabetes by giving pure lemon or musumbi juice to drink. Jaundice and clotting of arteries by cholesterol are alleviated by prolonged course of lemon juice. Many diseases of the respiratory system can be cured by including lemon juice in the diet. It may be sweetened by adding sugar to it.

Dr. Richard Lucas in his book 'Nature's Medicines' has expressed the view that lemons were highly valued in ancient times as medicine and for prevention of scurvy. Scurvy is a disease characterised by a spongy condition of the gums, loosening of the teeth, foul breath, debility and anaemia. There is also a tendency to haemorrhage especially into the mucous membranes and skin. Scurvy was common among the crewmen on the old time sailing vessels where the diet consisted entirely of dried or salted biscuits or loaf. The scientific answer to scurvy is vitamin C which is available in plenty in citrus fruits.

Drs. Wood and Ruddock in their book 'Encyclopaedia of health and home' remarked that lemon juice may be used in curing asthma, cough and cold, corns, headache, heartburn, vomiting and whooping cough.

Dr. M. Grieve in his book 'Modern Herbal' has said that washing the face with lemon juice and water is said to remove tan, freckles or blackheads.

Lemon juice rubbed in the scalp before shampooing is considered as an effective remedy for dandruff. A lemon milk preparation is employed for whitening and softening the skin of the hands and face. Lemon juice is an all-round beauty aid. Lemon juice makes a nice rinse for the hair. It will remove the soap film much better than plain water.

Dr. Joseph E. Meyer in his book 'Nature's Remedies' has said that a few drops of lemon juice sprinkled over sliced bananas, apples or grapes will prevent them from turning brown for a considerable period of time. Frequent applications of lemon juice is said to remove ink, rust, or mild stains from cloth.

For this purpose some recipes call for the addition of milk or salt to lemon juice.

Dr. A. N. Ghei in his book 'The Book of Food and Nutrition' has expressed that the addition of lemon juice to rice, boiled fish etc. gives a special flavour and has some specific action in promoting digestion. It is also used in salads. Being very rich in vitamin C, it acts as an antiscorbutic.

Dr. W. Hale-White in his book 'Materia Medica' has said that lemon-juice is used to relieve thirst and to make effervescing mixtures and drinks. Its action is the same as that of citric acid.

Nicholas Culpepper in his book 'Complete Herbal' has written that fruit and vegetable juice offers an excellent remedy for arthritis, bronchitis, intestinal disorders, stomach disorders and urinary disorders. He has observed that cooking destroys most of the natural vitamins and minerals. He has advised to consume raw fresh fruit and vegetable juices as far as practicable.

Harrison Dayal in his book 'Ancient Indian Energy Food' and Kristine Nolfi in her book 'My experiences with living food' have given various uses of lemon. Ramon Bernard in his book 'Herbal elixirs of life' has identified lemon as the 'miracle fruit'. Nelson Coon in his book 'Using plants for healing' has narrated the various medicinal uses of lemon.

3. Chebulic myrobalan (Haritaki):

Botanically it is known as Terminalia chebula. It contains tannins, chebulagic acid and gallic acid. It is a miraculous fruit having immense healing powers. Hippocrates said that if one bites a piece of haritaki after meals and swallows its juice, one will remain free from all diseases. Seven different types of haritaki are found and they are known as avaya, amrita, ketaki, juvanti, putana, vijoya and rohini. It is also known as 'long life elixir'. It is a magic fruit of proven value.

Haritaki chewed in the morning everyday in empty stomach heals a number of ailments like piles, colitis, skin eruptions, constipation, voice disorders, asthma, defective vision, wounds, acidity, gall-stones etc. The most important point to remember is that it increases longevity. It is said to be a good liver tonic.

It is one of three constituents of the well-known Indian preparation called triphala, the other two constituents are bahera and amlaki. Triphala is used as a laxative and in the treatment of enlarged liver, stomach troubles and pain in the eyes.

Haritaki increases appetite; if taken after boiling removes constipation; if taken after grinding, purifies blood; if taken along with other foods, increases intellect, vitality and sexual power; if taken after frying in ghee, it subsides vata, pitta, and kapha. Taken after principal meals, it prevents cough and cold, acidity, biliousness and stomach disorders.

Rules for taking haritaki in different seasons: During summer months, it should be taken with molasses; in rainy season, it should be taken with rock-salt; in autumn, it should be taken with sugar-candy; in dewy season, it is usually taken with ginger; in winter, it should be taken along with ground pepper and in spring, it is usually taken with honey.

Ayurvedic cures by haritaki

1. **Skin eruptions:** Haritaki juice subsides bile in the stomach. Skin troubles are usually caused by bile disorders. If its juice is taken daily after every principal meals, it cures all sorts of skin eruptions.

2. **Acidity:** Its juice neutralises too much acidity in the stomach if taken after all principal meals. It acts like miracle if taken with amalaki juice.

3. **Asthma:** Asthmatic tendencies can be reduced to the minimum by chewing a small piece of haritaki every night.

4. **Piles:** Piles can be easily cured if one takes a piece of haritaki before retiring to bed at night. It subsides the swollen veins of the walls of the anus.

5. **Gall-stones:** Gall-stones can be melted into water if one takes haritaki and amlaki juice daily after meals for some time.

6. **Eye troubles:** A mixture of haritaki and amlaki juices keeps the eyes healthy and strong.

A pregnant woman should not take haritaki as it may cause abortion.

J.F. Dastur in his book 'Medicinal Plants of India and Pakistan' has said that chebulic myrobalan is a mild, safe and efficacious laxative, astringent, stomachic, tonic, and alterative; the pulp of the fruit is given in piles, chronic diarrhoea, dysentery, costiveness, flatulence, asthma, urinary disorders, vomiting, hiccup, intestinal worms, ascites, enlarged liver and spleen.

4. Emblic myrobalan (Amlaki):

Botanically it is known as Emblica officinalis. It contains vitamin C, amino acid, tannin, polyphenolic compounds, fixed oil, lipids and essential oils. It may be compared to 'Amrita' of heaven because of its magical healing powers. It is also known as 'Long-life Elixir'. It is a tonic, laxative, and rejuvenative and it increases longevity. Hippocratés, the father of medicine, has said, 'If one bites a piece of amlaki and swallows its juice everyday, he will remain free from all sorts of diseases and he will be ever young'. Emblic myrobalan cures many ailments like acidity, septic fever, biliary colic, vomiting, insomnia, defective vision etc.

J.F. Dastur in his book 'Medicinal Plants of India and Pakistan' has said that the fruit is one of the richest sources of vitamin C; the fresh fruit is refrigerant, tonic, antiscorbutic, diuretic and laxative; it is used in fevers, hiccup, vomiting, indigestion, habitual constipation and other disorders of the digestive system. A decoction of the dried fruits is an efficacious douche in gonorrhoea; and an eye-wash in ophthalmia.

Dr. S.K. Jain in his book 'Medicinal Plants' has described the fruits as good liver tonic; raw fruits are cooling and mild laxatives. A fermented liquor made from the fruits is considered useful in indigestion, anaemia, jaundice, certain heart complaints, cold in nose and for promoting urination. It is a very rich source of vitamin C. Certain experiments on patients of pulmonary tuberculosis showed that vitamin C of emblic fruits is more quickly assimilated in the human system than synthetic vitamin C; perhaps there are certain unknown factors in the fruits responsible for this advantage. Dried fruits are useful in diarrhoea and dysentery.

Ayurvedic uses of amlaki

1. **High blood pressure:** Its juice is highly effective in reducing blood pressure and keeping it normal.

2. **Acidity:** It juice is highly effective in curing acidity permanently, if taken daily for a month.

3. **Defective vision:** Dim of vision can be restored to normal if its juice is taken daily after all principal meals.

4. **Septic fever:** Its juice is a household remedy for septic fever.

5. **Biliary colic:** Its juice is an age-old remedy for biliary colic.

6. **Insomnia:** It is very good for inducing sleep if its juice is taken before retiring to bed at night.

7. **Loss of hair (baldness):** Juice of Emblic myrobalan mixed with cocoanut oil may be applied on the hair-roots at night. It may stop further falling of hair and make the hair roots strong.

8. **Vomiting:** Its juice is very effective in curing all sorts of vomiting, nausea, car-sickness, travel-sickness and sea-sickness.

9. **Leucorrhoea:** The juice of amlaki is a very powerful remedy for leucorrhoea.

10. **Whooping cough:** It can be cured by taking amlaki juice with honey twice or thrice daily.

11. **Urinary and prostate gland disorders:** Its juice is highly effective in curing all sorts of urinary and prostate gland disorders.

5. Onion (Piyaj):

Botanically it is known as Allium cepa. It is a herbaceous biennial plant of the lily family (Liliaceae). Onion has a characteristic pungent aroma and sharp taste; it is used as a spice for many foods, particularly meats, sausages, vegetables and salads, and as a vegetable. Probably originating in the eastern

Mediterranean region and eastern Asia, the onion is unknown in the world state having been cultivated since prehistoric times. It is now grown all over the world but chiefly in the temperate zones.

The edible part consists of thickened leaf bases arising from the stem plate at the base of the build. The upper part of the leaf is hollow and cylindrical. A tuft of shallow, fibrous roots emerges from the stem plate. Onion powder is the spice consisting of the ground product of dehydrated trimmed onion bulbs. Onion salt is onion powder mixed with free running salt. Dehydrated flake onion and dehydrated instant minced onion are available. Dehydrated onion possesses the characteristic aroma and taste of fresh onion.

It is a fair source of vitamin C, organic sulphides, phenolic constituents, amino acids and essential oils. Many people do not realise that onion has many medicinal properties. Pliny listed no less than 33 ailments that could be cured by onion. The juice of the onion is one of the most irresistible antiseptics and disinfectants in the world; experiments in Russia showed that typhus, streptococci, staphylococci and masses of other organisms yielded to onion juice. Gangrene of wounds has been successfully treated by onion vapour in Russia. Onions are eaten raw as salad and boiled or baked in soups, curries, chutney and pickles. The pungency is due to the presence of a volatile oil allyl propyl disulphide.

J. F. Dastur in his book 'Medicinal Plants of India and Pakistan' has described the onion as a stimulant, diuretic, expectorant and rubefacient. As an emmenagogue and diuretic, it is eaten raw; its decoction is given in cough and strangury; cooked with vinegar the bulb is given in jaundice, splenic enlargement and dyspepsia; taken with salt it is a common remedy for colic and scurvy; onion is also used in obstruction of intestines. prolapse of the anus and as a sedative. As an emollient, crushed onion or its juice is applied over skin diseases and insect bites; its paste is applied with salt to unbroken chilblains; a poultice of the roasted bulb is used over indolent boils, wounds, broken chilblains, suppurating ears etc. Onion juice with mustard oil is applied as a liniment over painful joints, inflammatory swellings and skin diseases. A compress made of a roasted bulb applied to inflamed or protruded piles gives certain relief.

Dr. S. J. Singh in his book 'Practical Naturopathy' has described onions as one among the finest tonics we have. They are very useful in cases of fever, dropsy, catarrh and chronic bronchitis and mitigate cough of phthisis. If eaten raw at supper time, the onion ensures a good night's sleep. For a bad cold and cough there exists nothing better than the consumption of well-boiled or fried onions. Mixed with common salt, the onion is a common remedy in colic and scurvy. In malarial fevers, onions are eaten twice a day with 2-3 black-peppers with remarkable relief. Toothache is allayed by placing a small piece of onion on bad tooth or gum. In case of bleeding from the nose, an onion is cut in halves and placed in the neck. Warts also sometimes disappear if rubbed with cut onions. Roasted onions are applied as a poultice to indolent boils, bruises, wounds etc. to relieve heaty sensations and to bring the boil to maturity. In dysentery and body heat, they are applied to the navel. The juice of the roasted onion placed in the ear is an old remedy for earache.

He has also said that fresh onion juice promotes perspiration, relieves constipation and bronchitis; induces sleep. Onion juice is an excellent remedy for epilepsy. It is applied locally to allay irritation of insect bites, scorpion stings and bee stings. Embrocating bald patches on the head with its juice is said to promote growth of hair. Cooked with vinegar, they are given in jaundice, enlargement of spleen and dyspepsia. Onion juice dripped on cotton wool and put into the ear is a popular Russian remedy for noises in the ears. It is also dropped hot into the ear to relieve earache and applied hot to the soles of the feet as a derivative in convulsive disorders. It is sniffed in epistaxis and used like smelling salt in faintness, infantile convulsions, headaches, epileptic and hysterical fits. Mixed with mustard oil in equal proportions, it is a good application to rheumatic pains and other inflammatory swellings.

Joseph E. Meyer in his book 'Nature's Remedies' has said that onion has all the nutrients of wine and it vitalizes the body and makes it energetic. It has healing powers and cures many ailments of the body like cough and cold, nose-bleeding, sun-stroke, heat-stroke, allergy, hiccup, vomiting, boils and abscesses. It has special powers to keep the body cool in summer months if taken raw.

Sir R. N. Chopra in his book 'Indigenous Drugs of India' has said that onion juice is a popular remedy in cases of bronchitis, insomnia, cough and cold, sunstroke, heat-stroke, allergy, vomiting, boils and abscesses and jaundice.

K.R. Kirtikar in his book 'Indian Medicinal Plants' has said that onion juice is very useful in bronchitis, insomnia, cough and cold, sun-stroke, heat-stroke, vomiting, boil, abscess and liver troubles.

6. Margosa (Nim, neem):

Botanically it is known as Azadirachta indica. Almost every part of the tree is useful but the bark is perhaps the most useful. It is a good bitter tonic, astringent, antilithic and insecticidal. During autumn and spring seasons, the young leaves are eaten as a preventive against small-pox. The breeze of the margosa tree is very conducive to health. Juice of the leaves and bark has a miraculous healing power and it cures jaundice, worms, colic, eye troubles, indigestion, nightmares, vomiting, defective vision, blood poisoning and biliousness.

Ayurvedic medicinal uses of margosa leaves

Indigestion: Its bark juice cures indigestion and all sorts of liver troubles. Keep a piece of margosa bark in warm water at night and sip this water in the morning after filtering.

Nightmares: Bark juice with unboiled milk is a household remedy for nightmares.

Boil, abscess, carbuncle and tumour: The latex mixed with milk if taken every four hours daily helps to ripen, break and evacuate pus in the boils very neatly.

Jaundice: Leaf juice taken on empty stomach in the morning mixed with honey gives some relief.

Defective vision: Leaf juice is an age-old remedy for defective vision.

Worms: Dried and powdered margosa leaves may be taken on empty stomach with water.

Piles: 2 or 3 seeds of margosa may be chewed twice daily with water. This will certainly cure bleeding piles.

According to J. F. Dastur, the margosa leaves are carminative, expectorant, anthelmintic, antidotal, antilithic, diuretic and insecticidal; the fresh juice with salt is prescribed for intestinal worms; with money, the juice is given for jaundice and skin diseases. The tender twigs are chewed to keep the teeth and gums clean and healthy. An infusion of the flowers is administered in atonic dyspepsia and general debility. The fruit is usually recommended for urinary diseases, piles, intestinal worms and leprosy. Externally the oil is applied (extracted from the seeds) as an antiseptic dressing in leprosy, suppurating glands, uritcaria, chronic skin diseases like eczema, scabies, ringworm etc. A paste of the dried seeds is also used for killing head-lice.

Dr. S.K. Jain in his book 'Medicinal Plants' has described bark as a bitter tonic, astringent and antiperiodic. It is very useful in malarial fevers and skin disease. The leaves are bitter and are largely applied on skin diseases and boils.

Ayurvedic texts have described the various medicinal uses of margosa leaves, bark and seeds. The leaf juice is an effective remedy for malarial fever, skin eruptions, small-pox, chicken-pox, jaundice, diabetes, loss of appetite, and stomach disorders.

Chemically, it is composed of alkaloids, fatty acids and highly pungent essential oil.

7. Bitter-gourd (Karela):

Botanically it is known as Momordica charantia. It contains vitamin A, thiamine, riboflavin, nicotinic acid, vitamin C and iron. The fruit is very useful in gout, rheumatism, diseases of the spleen and liver. The fruit juice subsides vata, pitta and kapha the tridosas in ayurveda. The fruit and leaves are both administered orally in leprosy, piles and jaundice. Only the green fruit is used for medicinal purposes. The ripe fruit has got no value. Juice of the fresh leaves is also used as a mild purgative. The fruit is eaten by frying or boiling in cases of small-pox, chicken-pox and measles. With the advent of autumn and spring seasons, boiled fruit is eaten as a preventive against small-pox, chicken-pox and measles. Practically it acts as an anti-smallpox vaccine. The root is applied externally as pate to piles. The whole plant dried and powdered is used for dusting over the leprous and other intractable ulcers. Smaller varieties are richer in nutrients than larger ones. It is eaten boiled, baked, fried, stuffed and in curries and pickles.

According to J.F. Dastur, the leaf juice is anthelmintic, emetic and purgative; a decoction of the leaves is used as stomachic. The leaves are locally applied as a galactagogue; it is applied round the eyes for the cure of night blindness. The fruit is antidotal, antipyretic, tonic, appetizing, stomachic, anthelmintic, anti-bilious and laxative; it is used in leprosy, piles, jaundice, diabetes, rheumatism, gout, blood diseases, anaemia, urinary diseases, bronchitis and liver disorders; locally it is applied to burns, boils and eruptions.

8. Orange (Kamala lebu):

It is a citrus fruit. It contains vitamin C in adequate quantities. The tree of the sweet orange often grows to a height of 6 metres (20 ft.) and sometimes attains 10 metres (33 ft.). The broad, glossy, evergreen leaves are medium sized and ovate. Flowers are very fragrant. Although the usual shape of the sweet orange is round, certain varieties are greatly elongated and others much flattened. The pulp of the sweet orange is agreeably acidulous and sweet, the peel is comparatively smooth and oil glands are carved.

The fruit juice is an effective remedy for cough and cold, fever, scurvy, arthritis, rheumatism, gout, hypertension, sun-stroke, heat-stroke, nervous debility and menorrhagia.

According to Dr. H. Harold Home, sweet orange juice acts as a mild laxative, and it is very effective during cough and cold, fevers, general debility, dimness of vision, anaemia, lassitude, constipation, scurvy, and headache. It cures vomiting and checks car-sickness, It is very useful in low blood pressure.

9. Papaya (Papita or penpe):

Botanically it is known as Carica papaya. The fruit contains vitamin A, B, C. It is tonic, stomachic, stimulant, laxative, digestive, and rejuvenative. Ripe fruit is very useful in digestive disorders and if taken regularly, it cures all sorts of stomach troubles. The unripe fruit is also stomachic and digestive. The unripe fruit is prescribed in stomach troubles, jaundice, gastritis and liver disorders.

The papaya is a tropical melon-like fruit which grows in clusters. The tree grows to a height of 20 feet which is drowned by a tuft of leaves on long footstalks. The ripe fruit is yellowish orange and resembles a cantaloupe. It may be 4 to 20 inches (10 to 15 cm) long and weigh 1 to 10 pounds. It has a thick rind, fleshy pulp and many small black seeds.

It has a sweetish taste and is very rich in vitamins A, B and C. The juice of the papaya contains papain, a protein splitting enzyme used as a meat tenderizer.

Marcopolo credited the fruit with saving the lives of his sailors when they were attacked with scurvy. Vasco-da-Gama called papaya as the golden tree of life. Magellan regarded it as a valuable article of diet. Many of the ancient explorers found that the natives could tenderize tough meat or fowl by wrapping it in green papaya leaves overnight before cooking. Sometimes the juice or slices of unripe fruit were simply rubbed over the meat which served as a great meat tenderizer.

Richard Lucas in his book 'Nature's medicines' has said that the golden ripe papaya is generally recognised as a valuable health food. It is an excellent source of vitamins B and G. The green fruit is often stewed or baked and used as a substitute for squash. The unripe fruit as well as other parts of the plant contain a powerful protein digesting enzyme called pepsin which greatly resembles pepsin in its digestive action.

The crude papain of commerce is obtained by slashing the green fruits while they are still in the trees. The natural papain enzymes extracted from the unripe papaya melon has been extensively used in medicine industry and also as a meat tenderizer. It is also made into tablets and sold as a valuable aid for protein digestion. Everyone knows that as we grow older, the secretion of the natural juices in our bodies often declines causing incomplete digestion. This can result in gas, bloating, heartburn and stomach discomfort. These unpleasant symptoms may also occur among younger people whose digestion is disturbed by a sense of hurry, frustration, stress and strain. Papaya enzyme tablets aid in digesting the proteins of eggs, milk, meat, beans, and similar food products. Papain is also valued as an active blood-clotting agent and has been employed to arrest bleeding. It is also very useful in destroying intestinal worms.

Dr. M. Krigg in his book 'Green Medicines' has said that the ripe fruit is stomachic, appetizer, and digestive; it is given in piles and enlarged liver; the ripe fruit is eaten regularly for habitual constipation and chronic diarrhoea. The juice being an irritant is applied to swelling to prevent suppuration and to corns, warts, pimples, horny excretions of the skin and other skin diseases; the juice used as a cosmetic removes freckles and makes the skin smooth and delicate. A paste of the seeds is applied to skin diseases like ringworm.

Dr. S.J. Singh in his book 'Practical Naturopathy' has described papaya fruit as very useful in chronic diarrhoea; it is made into a curry and eaten by women to stimulate secretion of milk after childbirth. Slices of unripe fruit rubbed on the ringworm once daily is believed to cure it. The ripe fruit eaten regularly corrects habitual constipation, bleeding piles and dyspepsia. The leaves dipped in hot water or warmed over fire are applied to painful parts for relief from nervous pains. Bruised leaves applied as poultice are said to reduce elephantoid growths.

10. Marmelos/wood-apple (Bel):

Botanically it is known as Aegle marmelos. The wood-apple consists of fresh ripe, half-ripe fruits. Only the fruit is used as medicine. The marmelos fruit is very useful in curing diarrhoea and dysentery. Sherbets prepared from the pulp of the ripe fruit are soothing to intestines of patients who have just recovered from bacillary dysentery. The unripe or half-ripe fruits increase appetite and digestion. Bel morabbas are very useful in diarrhoea or dysentery.

Root: The root is generally worn as talisman or mascot on arms in order to overcome the evil influences of the sun which gives diseases like high fevers, inflammation, swellings, and the root is very effective in curing fevers, inflammatory complaints and swellings.

Fruit: The ripe fruit is very good for all sorts of stomach and liver troubles. The unripe fruit is also very good and is eaten as morabbas. It can be baked, roasted, stewed, or boiled or made into marmalades, jellies, tarts, pies, puddings, sauces etc. It is an age-old remedy for diarrhoea and dysentery.

Leaf: The leaf is given for reducing excessive sex urge, and sex perversions. The leaf juice is a favourite remedy for loss of memory and forgetfulness.

Dr. S.K. Jain in his book 'Medicinal Plants' has said that the ripe or unripe fruit is an age-old remedy for diarrhoea and dysentery. Marmalades made from unripe fruit is a sure remedy for dysentery.

R.N. Chopra in his book 'Indigenous Drugs of India' has said that the ripe or unripe fruit is a miraculous remedy for diarrhoea and dysentery. Marmalades made from the unripe fruit and taken daily during rainy season helps one to remain free from diarrhoea and dysentery.

J.F. Dastur in his book 'Medicinal Plants of India and Pakistan' has said the same thing.

11. Tomato (Bilati begun):

Tomato is a fruit of a cultivated plant belonging to the species Lycopersicum esculentum of the Nightshade family (Solanaceae) except for the tiny current tomato. Tomato plants are generally many branched, spreading 24 to 72 inches and recumbent when fruiting but a few forms are compact and upright. Leaves are more or less hairy, strong odorous, pinnately compound, up to 18 inches long. The flowers are yellow, 2 centimetres across, pendant and clustered. Fruits vary in diameter from half to 3 inches or more; they are usually red, scarlet or yellow; they vary in shape from almost spherical through oval and elongated to pear shaped. The fruit is soft, succulent, berry red or yellow in colour, containing two to many cells of small seeds surrounded by jelly-like pulp. It is used raw in salads, served as a cooked vegetable, used as an ingredient of various prepared dishes and pickles.

The tomato is a New World plant. It is a major crop in India, used fresh or canned for making a variety of sauces.

Since the plant requires warm weather and much sunlight, it is grown chiefly in hothouses in Great Britain and northern Europe. Tomatoes are the richest of all foods in vitamins. They are very rich in all three important vitamins like A, B and C while most vegetables are deficient in one or more. It is the most wonderful and effective blood cleanser known to man. It is rejuvenative, stomachic, stimulant, digestive and tonic. Unripe or half-ripe fruits are very effective in stomach disorders, liver troubles and spleen disorders. But excessive consumption may retard sexual desire. This is the main difficulty.

Dr. S.J. Singh in his book 'Practical Naturopathy' has described the tomato as very rich in food minerals which help to keep the blood alkaline and this maintain a high resistance to disease. It is very rich in iron and potash salts. Tomatoes stimulate torpid liver and are good in dyspepsia, diarrhoea and dysentery. It is purely a stomach and liver tonic.

Dr. C. C. Thakur in his book 'Introduction to Ayurveda' has said that it improves the digestive system and cures chronic diseases of the stomach. It is a blood purifier, cures anaemia, piles, liver troubles and chronic fever.

Dr. Amarnath Ghai has said that tomatoes contain all essential minerals, vitamin A, thiamine and vitamin C. These are used in salads, soups, ketchup, sauces and curries. It is an important protective food. Vitamin C of tomatoes is not destroyed by heat and therefore they are practically valuable for all sorts of stomach and liver troubles.

Dr. G. S. Verma in his book 'Miracles of fruits' has written that tomato is a sort of fruit and should better be taken uncooked. It is a nervine tonic and purifier of blood. It removes constipation and stengthens teeth. It is easily digestible and as such, it is recommended as a good diet for invalids and especially in fevers, diabetes and after long fasts. Being a rich source of vitamin A, it is a dependable preventive against eye troubles. It also contains a good amount of vitamin C and is a very effective preventive and curative of scurvy. It is also very good for stomach disorders. It contains not only vitamins A, B, C and G but also other minerals like iron, calcium, sulphur and potassium.

Medicinal uses of tomato:

Several medical books and journals have described medicinal uses of tomato. These are enumerated as under for ready reference:

1. **Blood-purifier:** Tomato juice keeps the blood stream alkaline and thus maintain a high resistance to disease. It is very rich in iron and potash salts.

2. **Liver troubles:** Half-ripe tomatoes offer an excellent remedy in all sorts of liver troubles. Tomatoes stimulate torpid liver and are very good for dyspepsia, diarrhoea and dysentery.

3. **Eye troubles:** Being a rich source of vitamin A, it is a dependable preventive against eye troubles.

4. **Nervous disorders:** Tomato is a nervine tonic. It is very useful in all sorts of nervous disorders.

5. **Scurvy:** As it is a rich source of vitamin C, it is very valuable in scurvy.

6. **Diarrhoea:** Half ripe tomatoes are very valuable in summer diarrhoea. But it should be taken with musumbi (lime) juice.

7. **Dysentery:** It is also very effective in dysentery. But it should be taken with garlic and musumbi (lime) juice.

8. **Sun-stroke:** Half-ripe tomatoes are very useful in hot summer months as it prevents sun-stroke or heat-stroke.

9. **Heartburn:** Tomatoes are usually effective in heartburn, flatulence or indigestion.

10. **Dyspepsia:** Half-ripe tomatoes are usually given in dyspepsia.

12. Tamarind (Imli, tentul):

Tamarind is botanically known as Tamarindus indica. It is also known as 'Jamdutika'. Chemically it contains vitamin C, tartaric acid, polysaccharide and oxalic acid. It is a tonic, carminative, laxative, digestive, febrifuge, refrigerant and antiseptic. It is very useful in habitual constiveness, alcoholic intoxication, dhatura poisoning, bilious vomiting, febrile disorders and dysentery. The tender leaves and flowers are eaten as vegetable which are very cooling and antibilious; their decoction is given to children as an anthelmintic; it is also useful in jaundice. A poultice of the fresh leaves is locally applied over inflammatory swelling of ankles and joints, sprains, boils, sore eyes and scabies. The pulp of the fruit is stimulant to the liver and cures digestive disorders. It is also very useful in curing burning sensation of the hands and feet during autumn and spring seasons.

Tamarinds are largely used in Indian cookery—in curries, salads and chutney. They contain vitamin C and are very useful in preventing and curing scurvy. The pulp of the ripe fruit is used in acute constipation and liver disorders like jaundice. The powdered seeds are given in dysentery. They are also applied locally for contracting the vaginal passage.

Dr. C.C. Thakur in his book 'Introduction to Ayurveda' has said that sweet tamarind subsides pitta (bile). It is an appetiser, digestive, stimulant to the liver, stomachic, good for heart and satisfies thirst. It is also good for retention of semen. It cures acidity, digestive disorders, dysentery, stomach troubles, arthritis, and all sorts of pains.

According to J.F. Dastur, the pulp of the ripe fruit is very useful in sun-stroke, heat-stroke, bilious fevers, alcoholic intoxication, dhatura poisoning, vomiting, car-sickness and travel sickness.

Ayurvedacharya Sivakali Bhattacharjee in his book 'Chiranjib Banaushadhi' has described tamarind as very useful in alcoholic intoxication, dhatura poisoning, sun-stroke, heat-stroke, allergy, loss of memory, bilious vomiting and bilious disorders.

Dr. S.K. Jain in his book 'Medicinal Plants' has said that the pulp of the ripe fruit is generally given in bilous fevers, vomiting, alcoholic intoxication, acute constipation, sun-stroke, and heat-stroke. It has got laxative properties. Its infusion in water forms a very refreshing drink in summer days.

13. Parbal (Patal):

Botanically it is known as Trichosanthes cucumberina. The plant is a cardiac tonic and antifebrile; its decoction is given in bilious fevers as a febrifuge and laxative. Chemically it contains saponin, hydrocarbons, sterols, glycoside and tannins. The fruit is digestive, stomachic and anti-bilious. Its main action is on the head and stomach. The root juice is a strong purgative. The leaf juice is emetic and so it should be taken with coriander to control bilious fever. The leaf juice is applied over the head for the cure of alopecia (baldness).

Ayurvedic medicinal uses of parbal:

Fevers: The plant is cardiac tonic and antifebrile. Its decoction with chirata and honey is given in bilious fevers as a febrifuge.

Boils and worms: A decoction or infusion of the plant is an efficacious remedy for boils and worms.

Baldness: The leaf juice is rubbed over the scalp for the cure of alopecia.

Ascites: Powder of the dried root is very effective in curing ascites.

Acidity: A decoction of its leaves with chebulic myrobalan taken in the morning on empty stomach is an age-old remedy for acidity and bilious disorders.

Liquor poisoning: Leaf juice is an age-old remedy for liquor poisoning.

Blood pressure: Leaf juice is a household remedy for controlling high blood pressure.

14. Cucumber (Sasha, khirika):

It is a creeping plant of the cucurbitaceae family probably originating in India and widely cutivated for its fruit. It is a tender annual with a rough, succulent trailing stem and hairy leaves with 3 to 5 pointed lobes; the stem bears branched tendrils, by which the plant creeps through the supports.

The food value of cucumber is low; but it is popular for salads and relishes. Fresh cucumber should be firm, well-shaped and bright green in colour. They may be kept in refrigerated storage for about 2 weeks.

It is a very favourite fruit during hot summer months as it keeps the body cool and calm. It subsides pitta (bile) and aids digestion. It prevents sun-stroke, heat-stroke and allergy. It quenches thirst.

15. Apple (Apel):

It is a fruit of the genus Malus (about 25 species) belonging to the family Rosaceae, the most widely cultivated fruit tree. The apple is one of the fleshy fruits in which the ripened ovary and surrounding tissue both become fleshy and edible. The apple flower of most varieties requires cross pollination for fertilisation and a desirable fruit set by 2% to 3% bloom. The apple at harvest though varying widely in shape, size, colour and acidity depending upon the environmental character is nevertheless usually roundish 50 to 100 millimetres (1 to 4 inches) in diameter and some shade of red or yellowish in colour.

There are thousand varieties of apples but it can be divided into three main classes viz. cider varieties, cooking varieties and dessert varieties. They differ widely but tend to emphasize colour, size, aroma, smoothness and perhaps crispness and tang. Many are relatively high in sugar, only mildly acidic and very low in tannin. The apple thrives in favourable localities from approximately 30° to 80° latitude north and south.

Apples provide vitamin A and C, are very high in carbohydrates and are an excellent source of cellulose. In Europe, a larger fraction of the crop goes for cider, wine and brandy. Of the total production, one fourth goes for cider.

When eaten raw, the apple is used as common food or as dessert at meals. It can be baked, roasted, stewed or boiled or made into marmalades, jellies, tarts, pies, puddings, cakes, sauces and apple butter.

Apple-jack is the name given in the United States to apple-brandy. In France, brandy distilled from apples is a popular drink; it is called Calvados. It received its name from the Department of Calvados in Normandy, a centre of French apple production. Apple-jack is sold after it has aged from 2 to 5 years. Calvados usually is aged for 10 years.

There is an age-old proverb : 'An apple a day keeps the doctor away'. It means that if one eats one apple a day, he will remain free from all diseases. Such is the food value of apples. It is valuable in cases of anaemia, high fever, general debility, lassitude, arthritis, pimples, bad blood and low vitality.

16. Pineapple (Anaras):

It is a fruit bearing plant of the family Bromeliaceae native to tropical and sub-tropical regions. The pineapple plant resembles the agave or some yuccas in general appearance. It has 30 to 40 stiff succulent leaves closely spaced in a rosette on a thick, fleshy stem. With commercial varieties, a determinate inflorescence forms about 15 to 20 months after planting in a flower stock 100 to 150 mm (4 to 6 inches) in length. The original separate lavender flowers together with their bracts, each attached to a central axis core, become fleshy and fuse to form the pineapple fruit which ripens in five to six months, after flowering begins. Fruits of commercial varieties range from one to two kg (2 to 4 pds) in weight.

When pineapple is cultivated on plantation, an asphalt impregnated mulch paper is first laid on well-tilled soil in rows with the edges covered to anchor the stripes of paper. The pineapple propagating pieces are inserted through the paper to the soil, so spaced as to give a population of 15,000 to 20,000 plants per acre. In many cases, the soil is fumigated to kill parasitic nematodes on the roots of the plants.

The fruit contains vitamin C, iron and other minerals. It acts as an effective laxative. It is a tonic and rejuvenative. Juice of the unripe fruit causes uterine contractions and should not be given to a pregnant woman. Juice of the ripe fruit cures gastric irritability in fever and is very helpful in jaundice.

Florence Daniel in her book 'Food Remedies' has named pineapple juice as the specific remedy for diphtheria. The ripe fruit is very useful in sore throat, bowel disorders and acute constipation.

17. Banana (Kela, kala):

It is an important fruit consumed extensively throughout the tropics, where it is grown and also valued in temperate zones for its flavour, food value and availability throughout the year.

Banana belongs to the genus Musa of the family Musaceae. The plant, a gigantic herb springing from an underground stem or rhizome, forms a false trunk 3 to 6 metres (10 to 20 ft.) high composed of the leaf sheaths and crowned with a rosette of 10 to 20 oblong to elliptic leaves sometimes attaining a length of 3 to 3-1/2 metres (10 to 11-1/2 ft.) and a breadth of 650 millimetres (26 inches).

The large flower spike carrying numerous yellowish flowers emerges at the top of the false trunk and bends downwards to become bunches of 50 to 150 individual fruits in clusters or hands of 10 to 20. After the plants have fruited, they die and are replaced by others arising from the underground stem. The life of one stool or clump thus continues for many years.

There are 100 or more varieties of banana in cultivation; confusion exists because of diverse names applied to one and the same variety in different parts of the world.

Desirable commercial bunches of bananas consist of nine hands or more and weigh 22 to 65 kg. The ripe fruit contains as much as 22% carbohydrates, mainly as sugar and is high in ash, low in protein and fat and a good source of vitamin C.

Cooking varieties or plantains differ from other bananas in that the ripe fruit is starchy rather than sweet. The fruit is demulcent, aphrodisiac and stomachic. As an astringent, it is given in dysentery. An ounce of the ripe fruit mixed with tamarind and salt is a household remedy in early cases of diarrhoea and dysentery. The fruit is also useful to relieve soreness of throat and chest accompanied with dry cough. It is also taken to correct irritability of the bladder. The ripe fruit is a mild laxative. The unripe fruit is very good for all sorts of stomach and liver troubles, including gastric ulcer. The flour of the dried fruit is prescribed in diarrhoea, dysentery and dyspepsia. The unripe fruit is very useful in diabetes and spitting of blood.

The juice of the flowers is given with curds in menorrhagia and diabetes. Those who are suffering from cough and cold, dyspepsia, obesity and diabetes should not eat the ripe fruit. The unripe fruit can be eaten boiled, stewed and in curries etc.

18. Beet:

It is the cultivated form of the plant Beeta vulgaris of the Goosefoot family (Chenopodiaceae), one of the most important vegetables. Four different types are cultivated for four different purposes viz. 1. the garden beet or beet-root or table-beet as a garden vegetable, 2. the sugar-beet, a major source of sugar, 3. the mangel-wurzel or mangold, a succulent beet for livestock and 4. The leaf-beet or Swiss chard for its leaves which may be eaten or used as a seasoning.

The garden beet is grown for the thick, fleshy taproot that forms during the first season. In the second season, a tall branched leafy stem arises to bear cluster of minute green flowers that develop into brown corky fruits commonly called seedballs. The taproot ranges in shape from flattened oblate, though globular and somewhat conical to long tapered skin and flesh; colours are usually dark to dark-purplish red, with some nearly white.

Beet-root grows in deep, friable soils that are high in organic matter; they respond well to chemical fertilisers and manures. Beet greens, a rich source of riboflavin, iron and vitamins A and C are frequently served in cooked form. The tops of red garden beets and the foliage of Swiss chard used as greens are excellent sources of vitamins A and B1 and B2. Beet offers an excellent remedy for anaemia, general debility, low vitality, lassitude and nervous debility. But in India it is not good to consume beet during hot summer months as it may cause high blood pressure and insomnia. But in winter months, it may be taken to keep the body warm. It is prized as a nervine tonic. Red beet juice is highly effective in dissolving fibroid tumours.

Dr. John B. Lust has prescribed 16 ounces of raw carrot and beet juice for tumour patients. He has advised that our meals should consist of some fresh raw fruit such as apple, grapes, pears, narangis, pineapples and shaddock. This combination of fresh fruits and the raw juices will generally provide the much needed stimulus for normal bowel movement.

19. Carrot (Gajar):

It is a herbaceous, generally biennial plant of the Apiaceae family that produces an edible taproot. Among common varieties, root shapes range from globular to long, with ends blunt to long pointed. Besides the orange coloured roots, white-yellow and purple-fleshed varieties are known.

The plants require cool to moderate temperatures and are not grown in summer in the warmer regions. They require deep, rich and losely packed soil. Fresh carrots should be firm and crisp with smooth and unblemished skin. Bright orange colour indicates high carotene content; smaller types are the most tender. Carrots are used in salads and as relishes and are served as cooked vegetable and in stews. Carrots are rich sources of vitamins A, B and C. They also contain minerals and organic acids.

Carrot juice is highly effective in all sorts of fevers, general debility, nervous disorders, anaemia, lassitude, low vitality, and run-down conditions. It should not be taken during hot summer months as it may cause insomnia and high blood pressure. During winter months, carrots may be eaten in order to keep the body warm and to fight cold.

Dr. John B. Lust has said, 'Carrot juice is sometimes called miracle juice. A large number of people in all walks of life suffering from various ailments have found that the inclusion of carrot juice in their diet has greatly improved their health'.

Dr. J.J. Schiffers has said, 'Vitamin A promotes growth of bones and teeth, the maintenance of healthy body tissues and glandular functions. It aids in the resistance to infection. Vitamin A is especially necessary in the diet of expectant mothers to build up and maintain the health of both mother and the developing child. Fresh carrot juice should be included in the diet not only during pregnancy but also during the period of nursing the baby. Carrot juice is one of the richest source of vitamin A'.

Dr. Harry Benjamin has said, 'Carrot juice is the rich source of vitamin E which is very helpful in case of cancer. In laboratory tests, when the cancer tissue was placed in a vitamin E rich blood stream, it did not grow. When a blood serum lacking vitamin E was used in a similar test, the cancer cells grew readily.' This test proved that carrots are very valued to cancer patients.

20. Soyabean:

It is a annual summer leguminous plant, native to eastern Asia; economically the most important bean in the world. The soyabean is an erect, branching plant, resembling in its early growth ordinary field beans. Varieties range in height from 30 centimetres to 2 metres. The deep roots are responsible in part for the great resistance to drought offered by soyabeans.

The seeds are usually yellow green, brown or black but may be bicoloured. No truly white or red seeds are known. The commonest bicoloured patterns are green or yellow with a saddle-like patch of black or brown extending down on each side of hilum or seed scar. The soyabean succeeds on nearly all types of soils but does best on fertile or sandy loams.

Soyabeans which are low in starch and high in fat and protein are sometimes used as a meat substitute. Most U.S. soyabeans are made into oil and meal. The oil is principally used for food and also in paint, chemical and other industries.

Apart from eating them as cooked vegetables, we can make a flour of soyabeans and use it for the relief of swollen testicles, swollen breasts and to the eyelids where there is excessive watering of the eyes.

21. Coconut (Narikel or nariyel):

It is a tree of the palm family (Arecaceae). It is one of the most important crops in the tropics. The slender, leaning, ringed trunk of the tree rises to a height of upto 80 ft. (25 metres) from a swollen base and is surmounted by a graceful crown of giant, feather-like leaves. Flowering begins in trees five-year-old and is continuous thereafter. Fruits require a year to ripen; the annual yield per tree may reach 100 but 50 is considered good. Mature fruits, ovoid or ellipsoid in shape, 100 to 450 millimetres (12 to 18 inches) in length and 150 to 200 millimetres (6 to 8 inches) in diameter, have a thick, fibrous husk surrounding the familiar single seeded nut of commerce. A hard shell encloses the insignificant embryo with its abundant endosperm, composed of both meat and liquid.

Coconut palms flourish best close to the sea or low lying areas a few feet above high water where there is circulating ground water and an ample rainfall. The harvested coconut yields copra; the dried kernel or meat from which coconut oil, the world's high ranking vegetable oil, is extracted. Coconut oil has many uses like manufacture of soaps and shampoos, detergents, edible oils, margarines, vegetable shortenings, synthetic rubber, glycerine, hydraulic fluid and plasticizer. Copra meal is a livestock feed and fertilizer and shredded coconut is a familiar item on grocer's shelves. Besides the edible kernels and the drink obtained from the green-nuts, the husk yields coir, a fibre highly resistant to salt water and used in the manufacture of ropes, mats, baskets, brushes and brooms.

Other useful products derived from the coconut palm include toddy, palm-cabbage and construction materials. The liquid inside green nuts offers a refreshing drink during hot summer months which keeps the body cool. It subsides pitta and prevents sun-stroke, heat-stroke and vomiting. It is given in thirst, fever and uninary disorders; it is a blood purifier and checks travel sickness and nausea. The milky juice expressed from the pulp of the immature nut is nutritive and anthelmintic. It is very useful in malnutrition, general debility, fevers and urinary disorders. The liquid inside the ripe nut is highly diuretic and so should be taken only in small doses.

22. Cashew nut (Kaju-badam):

It is an edible seed or nut of Anacardium occidentale family, a tropical and sub-tropical evergreen shrub or tree up to 12 metres (40 ft.) growing where the soil is fertile and the humidity high. The tree is chiefly important for the nuts it produces but it also produces wood for making shipping crates, boats, charcoal etc. and a gum similar to gum arabic.

The nut shaped like a large thick bean is sometimes more than 2.5 centimetres (one inch) long and forms in an unusual way. It appears as though one of its ends had been forcibly sunk into the calyx end of a fleshy, pear-shaped fruit called the cashew apple which is about 3 times as large as the nut and reddish or yellow. The cashew apple is used locally in beverages, jams and jellies. The nut has two walls or shells. The fruits are picked by hand and the nuts are first detached then sun-dried.

The fruit is prescribed in scurvy and diarrhoea. Its juice is a powerful diuretic and is used in uterine complaints and dropsy. It is a useful local application in neuralgic and rheumatic pains. The nut is specially useful in acute cases of impotency as it increases sexual vigour considerably. The oil extracted from the shell of the nut is applied to warts, corns, psoriasis and ringworm.

23. Pomegranate (Dalim):

It is a fruit of Punica granatum, a bush or small tree. The plant may attain 5 or 7 metres (16 or 23 ft.) in height, has elliptic to lance shaped bright green leaves and handsome axillary orange-red flowers borne toward the ends of the bracelets. The fruit is the size of a large orange obscurely six-sided with a smooth, leathery skin that ranges from brownish yellow to red; within it is divided into several chambers containing many thin, transparent vesicles or reddish juicy pulp each surrounding an angular and elongated seed. It is said, 'Eat pomegranate for it purges the system of envy and hatred.' Though the pomegranate grows in a wide range of climates, good fruit is produced only where cool temperature and dry atmosphere accompany the ripening period.

The fruit contains vitamins B and C along with citric acid. The acid saccharine juice from the fresh fruit is of great value in dyspepsia and also forms an excellent cooling beverage in cases of fevers and sickness, quenching thirst. The syrup prepared from the fruit is also a cooling drink and very useful in all sorts of bilious complaints. The fruit juice mixed with clove or cinnamon is prescribed in acute bronchitis, sore throat and typhoid. It is also used in uterine ulcers and uterine disorders. A fluid extract of the fresh bark is also useful in expelling worms. The flower juice is sometimes used as snuff in nose-bleeding. The fruit juice with honey is sometimes given in loss of memory. The fruit juice increases memory and for this reason, it is very useful for students.

Ayurvedic medicinal uses of pomegranate juice:

Dysentery: The juice of the fresh leaves and young fruit is given in dysentery.

Conjunctivitis: A paste of the leaves is locally used in conjunctivas.

Fever: The root-bark is given as a febrifuge in fevers. The fruit juice quenches thirst and acts as cooling agent.

Spleen enlargement: Dried pomegranate root juice with milk is prescribed in spleen enlargement, and general debility.

Leucorrhoea: The flower buds are given in acute cases of leucorrhoea, diarrhoea and dysentery.

Typhoid: A sherbet of the ripe fruit is given in typhoid fever, gastric and asthmatic fevers.

Urinary disorders: The fruit juice is highly effective in urinary disorders.

High blood pressure: The fruit juice is highly effective in reducing high blood pressure.

Loss of memory: The fruit juice with honey is an age-old remedy for loss of memory.

Worms: Dried powdered root mixed with lime-water is prescribed for expelling worms.

Diarrhoea and dysentery: The rind of the fruit is known as dalim chhal and this is very useful in intermittent fever, diarrhoea and dysentery.

Nose-bleeding: The flower juice is often prescribed in nose-bleeding to be taken as snuff.

24. Cherry:

It is well-known for flavouring. Three types of cherry are mainly grown for their fruit. These are the sweet cherries, the sour cherries and the dukes. The fruit is usually globular shaped, about 2 centimetres (1 inch) in diameter and varies in colour from yellow to red. The acid content of the sweet cherry is low; the higher acid content of the sour cherries produces characteristic tart flavour. Sour cherry trees are smaller, rarely 5 metres (16 ft.) in height.

The fruits of all varieties provide very small amounts of minerals like calcium and phosphorus. It is used fresh, canned or for wine. Cherry wine is very popular among European people. The fruit is used in Indian sweets for flavouring purposes.

25. Dates (Khejur):

Date-palm is a tree of the Phoenix dactylifera of the palm family. The date-palm grows about 23 metres (75 ft) tall and its stem is strongly marked with pruned stubs of old leaf bases, terminates in a crown of graceful, shining, pinnate leaves about 5 metres long. Male and female flowers are borne on separate plants. Under cultivation, the female flowers are artificially pollinated. The date is a one-seeded fruit or berry usually oblong but varying in shape, size, colour, quality and consistency of flesh according to the condition of culture. More than 1000 dates may appear in a single bunch weighing 8 kg or more. The dried fruit is more than 50% sugar by weight and contains about 2% each of protein, fat and mineral water. Syrup, alcohol, vinegar and strong liquor are derived from the fruit. The sap is also used as a beverage either fresh or fermented but because the method of extraction seriously injures the palm, only those trees that produce little fruit are used for sap. When a palm is cut down, the tender terminal bud is eaten as salad. Date-sugar, a commercial product of India, is obtained from the sap of a closely related species Phoenix sylvestris.

The fresh fruit is nutritious, tonic and mild laxative. It contains vitamins A and B, calcium, iron, potassium, phosphorus and alkaloids. Its infusion with milk is nourishing and restorative tonic; for this reason it is given during convalescence from fevers and small-pox. The fruit is very good for cough and cold, asthma, laryngitis, chest complaints, fevers, dysentery and liver complaints. Taking dates with milk early in the morning during winter months is found to be a better tonic than other ordinary tonics and is very easily available at that time. Syrup prepared from dates is also useful in cases of diarrhoea, marasmus, diabetes insipidus.

26. Grape-fruit or shaddock (Batabi lebu or jamburi):

It is a medium size chiefly sub-tropical tree of the Citrus family (Rutaceae) and it is an edible fruit. The grape-fruit tree bears leathery, evergreen leaves and white flowers and often attains a height of 30 ft. (9 mtrs) or more. Its globular fruit, rich in vitamins B and C, is a modified berry known botanically as a hesperidium. It has a thick, smooth, pale yellow peel and a juicy acid. The fruit 4 to 6 inches in diameter is the largest of the citrus fruits.

The fruit juice is a very effective remedy in acute constipation, arthritis, gout, sciatica, oedema, and high blood pressure. Externally the fruit juice cures corns, skin diseases and freckles. The fruit juice with milk is often prescribed for whitening the skin and softening of hands and feet. The fruit is also given in vomiting, sea or travel sickness.

Dr. H. Harold Hume in his book 'Citrus fruits' has said that the grape-fruit juice is very helpful in acute constipation, vomiting, travel sickness, gout, sciatica, arthritis and high blood pressure.

27. Grape (Angur):

It is a member of the grape genus vitis (family Vitaceae) with about 60 species native to the north temperate region, including variations that may be eaten as table fruit, dried to produce raisins or crushed to make grape wine. In wine-making, Vitis vinifera is commonly used.

In North America, the grape is a woody vine climbing by means of tendrils (modified branches) and when untrained often reaching a length of 17 metres (56 ft) or more. In arid regions, it may form an almost erect shrub. The leaves are alternate, palmately lobed and always two-edged. Small greenish flowers in clusters, precede the fruit which varies in colour from almost black to green, red and amber. Botanically the fruit is a berry more or less globular within juicy pulp of which lie the seeds. In many varieties, the fruit is covered with a whitish powder bloom. All grapes contain sugar (glucose and fructose) in varying quantities depending upon the variety.

Grape culture or viticulture is nearly as old as man. Noah planted a vineyard. In Homer's time, wine was a regular commodity among the Greeks. Pliny, the elder, described 91 varieties of grapes, distinguished 50 kinds of wine and described vine training methods.

The mature fruit of all varieties may ferment into a kind of wine when crushed and most groups can be dried or eaten fresh. But only a limited number of varieties produce standard or higher quality wines, three varieties account for most of the raisins of commerce, only 15 to 20 varieties are grown extensively as table grapes.

Grape jelly is often made from grape juice both commercially and in the home. For grape jelly, concorn is the favoured variety. Raisins have been made for many centuries by drying suitable varieties of grapes. Raisins have a sugar content of 66% to 72%.

Grape contains a number of vitamins, iron and minerals. It is prescribed in acute constipation, fevers, liver and stomach troubles. It is a tonic, rejuvenative and refresher.

28. Lime (Musumbi):

Lime contains vitamins A, B, C, G and rare vitamin P. It also contains various other minerals and acids. The fruit juice is an efficacious remedy in scurvy, anaemia, intestinal disorders, cough and cold, gastric troubles, constipation, fevers, typhoid and high blood pressure. It is a tonic, rejuvenative and refresher.

Of all fruits, musumbi is called the miracle fruit. If one takes a musumbi a day, he will remain free from all sorts of diseases. It has got great powers to wash away waste products from inside the body.

Lime is a citrus fruit. The lime tree (Citrus aurantifolia) belongs to the Rue family (Rutaceae). Its fruits like other citrus fruits are very rich in vitamins A, B and C. They have a tangy flavour and are used in cooking, baking, pickling etc.

The lime tree has glossy, elliptical or oblong leaves usually 2 to 3 inches long. The tiny white flowers are usually borne in small clusters. The fruit is a type of berry known as a hesperidum. It has juicy pulp divided into several compartments and a thick rind containing oil glands.

This fruit originated in Malaysia and its neighbouring regions. But it was reported in Europe by the 13th century but limes were not popular there until the 17th century. In the 18th century, seamen on British sailing vessels ate limes to prevent scurvy and the sailors became popularly known as 'Limeys'.

The lime tree was grown in plenty in Haiti having been introduced there by Columbus in 1433. It then became naturalised throughout West Indies, along the coast of Mexico and on the Florida Keys. Today the world's chief areas of lime production are Egypt, India, Mexico and the West Indies.

The fruit is very rich in vitamins A, B and C. It also contains minerals. This fruit is very valuable in liver and stomach troubles, bronchitis, cough and cold, sore throat, pharyngitis, laryngitis, diarrhoea, dysentery and spleen troubles.

Cough and cold : It is an age-old remedy in cough and cold.

Anaemia and general debility: Musumbi juice is very effective in anaemia and general debility.

Forgetfulness: Its juice increases memory and gives vitality.

High blood pressure: The fruit juice is highly effective in keeping the blood pressure normal.

Intestinal disorders: Musumbi juice is often prescribed in all sorts of intestinal disorders.

Jaundice: Musumbi juice is an age-old remedy for jaundice.

Gastric or peptic ulcer: It is the only fruit juice which can cure gastric ulcer most effectively.

Menorrhagia: It is a very effective remedy for menorrhagia.

Kidney disorders: Narangi juice cures all sorts of kidney disorders. It is a miracle fruit.

Nausea, vomiting and travel sickness: Musumbi juice is very effective in curing all sorts of travel sickness.

Diarrhoea and dysentery: Musumbi juice is an effective remedy in diarrhoea and dysentery.

Flatulence and indigestion: Its juice is very effective in flatulence or indigestion.

Sun-stroke or heat-stroke: In hot summer months, narangi juice gives protection against any possible sun-stroke or heat-stroke.

Dr. H. Harold Hume in his book 'Citrus Fruits' has said that musumbi juice is very effective in all sorts of stomach, liver and spleen troubles. It cures diarrhoea and dysentery very quickly. Jaundice can be easily cured if one drinks a cup of musumbi juice in the morning.

R. B. Duckworth in his book 'Fruits and Vegetables' has said that musumbi juice is an effective remedy for all sorts of stomach and liver troubles. It may be called a miracle fruit.

Fred. E. Deatherage in his book 'Food for Life' has described musumbi juice as a household remedy for stomach and liver troubles. F. Ramalay in his book 'Plants useful to man' has said that musumbi juice is a very effective remedy for all sorts of stomach and liver troubles. It may be called 'heal-all'.

29. Pear (Naspati):

It is a member of Pyrus communis of the rose family (Rosaceae). It is mainly cultivated in temperate zones. The pear tree is broad-headed and up to 13 metres (43 ft.) high at maturity; it is taller and more upright than the apple tree. The roundish to oval, leathery leaves, somewhat wedge-shaped at their bases appear about the same time as the flowers which are 25 millimetres (1 inch) wide and usually white. The pear flowers form groups of 5 to 8 in erect corymbs and are generally white or pinkish.

Pears are generally sweeter and of softer texture than apples. The fruit is distinguished by the presence of hard cells in the flesh, the so called grit or stone cells which are absent in apples. Pear fruits are elongated being narrow at the stem end and broader at the opposite end.

Pear trees are relatively long living (50 to 75 years) and may reach considerable size unless carefully trained and pruned. Within 4 to 7 years of setting out, the tree begins to bear fruits at the age of 20 to 25; It should yield 25 to 45 bushels of fruit. Fruits are consumed fresh or cooked in various ways. The fermented juice of the pear, corresponding to cider made from apples, is called 'Perry' (a type of wine).

Italy is the largest producer of pears. Then comes China which produces 11% of the world production. Pear contains various vitamins and minerals. It is given in anaemia, general debility, fevers, diarrhoea, dysentery, cough and cold.

30. Potato (Alu):

A herbaceous plant belonging to the tomato, tobacco and deadly nightshade family (Solanaceae). The potato, white potato, common potato or Irish potato, is one of the main food crops of the world, differing from others in that the edible part of the plant is a tuber, i.e. the swollen end of an underground stem.

It is a herbaceous plant 50 to 100 centimetres (20 to 40 inches) high. Leaf arrangement is spiral; underground stems (stolons) extend from the stem below ground. The ends of the stolons may enlarge greatly from a few to many tubers of variable shape and size usually ranging in weight up to 300 gm, occasionally purple. The tubers bear spirally arranged buds (eyes) in the axils of aborted leaves of which scars remain.

Potatoes are frequently served whole or mashed as cooked vegetable and are also ground into potato flour, used in baking and as a thickener for sauces. Potatoes containing starch are highly digestible. They also supply vitamin C, amino acids, protein, thiamin and nicotinic acid.

The juice of raw potato if applied externally may relieve rheumatic pain and a crushed potato can be applied to sore or wound, bandaged and to be changed twice daily. The housewife who burns herself in the kitchen will find quick relief if she applies a little crushed potato to the burn. It is not good to eat potatoes in excess. It is not good for high blood pressure patients. Diabetic patients are not advised to eat potatoes.

31. Guava (Peyara):

It is a fruit of the genus Psidium (family Myrtaceae). The common guava is a large shrub or small tree with quadrangular branchlets, oval to oblong leaves about 7.6 centimetres (3 inches) in length and four-petalled white flowers about 2.5 centimetres broad. The fruits are round to pear shaped and measure up to 7.6 centimetres in diameter; the white to salmon-red pulp contain many such hard seeds.

Guavas are processed into jams, jellies and preserves. Fresh guavas are rich in vitamins A, B and C; they are eaten raw or sliced and served with sugar and cream as a dessert. It is highly effective in removing constipation. It is commonly called 'Indian apple'.

32. Water-melon (Tarmuj):

It is a trailing fleshy vine of the gourd family (Cucurbitaceae), native to tropical Asia but grown in many warm countries for its edible fruit. It has solitary yellow flowers 7.5 to 10 centimetres (3 to 4 inches) wide; hairy oval leaves that are heart shaped at the base and a melon-shaped or cucumber shaped fruit 20 to 38 centimetres (8 to 15 inches) long. Each green fruit has whitish waxy covering and contains fat, white seeds about half inch long.

Water-melon juice is a very favourite and refreshing drink in hot summer months. It subsides pitta, keeps the body cool and calm. It prevents sun-stroke and heat-stroke. It is a tonic, digestive and rejuvenative.

33. Lichi (Lichu):

It is a fruit of Litchi chineasis, a tree of the family Sapindaceae. The handsome tree develops a compact crown of bright-green foliage. The leaves are compound, composed of 2 to 4 pairs of elliptic to lanceolate leaflets 2 or 3 inches long. The flowers, small and inconspicuous, are borne in loose diverse terminal clusters or panicles sometimes 30 centimetres (12 inches) in length. The fruits which are produced in clusters are oval to round, strawberry red in colour and about 25 millimetres in diameter. The brittle outer covering encloses white, translucent watery flesh and one large seed. The flavour is subacid. The fruit is eaten fresh, canned or dried. It is usually available in summer months. It subsides pitta. It is mild laxative. The fruit is given in acute constipation. It keeps the body cool and calm. It prevents sun-stroke and heat-stroke.

34. Mangosteen (Gab):

Botanically it is known as Diospyros peregrina. It is a beautiful, delicious fruit of tropical southeast Asia produced by a handsome tree that under favourable conditions can reach a height of 9.5 metres (31 ft). It has thick, dark, green glossy leaves; the flowers are large and polygamous. The fruits are about 3 inches in diameter, round to oblate in form and dark purple in colour. They have thick, hard rinds surrounding a large cavity in which is found snow-white flesh in segments resembling those of a mandarine orange. The mangosteen is juicy, delicate in texture and of delightful, slightly tart flavour.

Ayurvedic uses of mangosteen

A decoction of the bark is a household remedy for chronic dysentery, diarrhoea, menorrhagia and intermittent fever. A poultice of the bark is a applied to boils and abscesses. The fruit is also given in diarrhoea, dysentery and menorrhagia. In asthma, the dried rind of the fruit is smoked in doses of 45 grain.

An extract of the fruit juice prepared by evaporating it on water bath to dryness is a very useful remedy for chronic diarrhoea and dysentery. An infusion of the bark is an effective gargle in sore throat, and mouth disorders.

35. Fig (Dumur):

It is a plant of the genus Ficus of the mulberry family (Moraceae). Ficus carica (the common fig) which yields the well-known fig of commerce is indigenous to an area extending from Asiatic Turkey to India. It is a bush or small tree from a metre to 12 metres high with broad, rough, deciduous leaves, deeply lobed.

Fig fruits are borne singly or in pairs above the scars of fallen leaves or in axils of leaves. The flowers are male or female. The fig is one of the earliest fruit trees cultivated by primitive man. Figs are known to possess in an unusual degree two important food qualities : a definite laxative effect and a high alkalinity of ash. The laxative effect is probably due to the bulk of seeds and fibre combined with some specific solvent present in the juice. In Mediterranean countries, the fig is so widely used both fresh and dried that it is called 'the poor man's food'.

Figs provide such minerals as calcium and phosphorus; dried figs are also high in iron. The figs are astrigent and carminative; the dried figs are given in doses of 150 gram with honey in menorrhagia, hepatitis and dysentery; the figs are very useful in diabetes; A decoction of dried figs is an excellent mouthwash for sore throat and aphthous complaints of the mouth.

36. Nutmeg (Jaiphal):

It is a spice consisting of the seed of the Myristica fragens, a tropical dioecious evergreen tree native to Moluccas of Spice Islands of Indonesia. Nutmeg has a characteristic, pleasant fragrance and slightly warm taste; it is used to flavour many kinds of baked goods, confections, puddings, meats, sausages, sauces, vegetables and beverages.

The trees may reach about 65 feet (20 metres) tall. They yield fruit 8 years after sowing, reach their prime in 25 years and bear fruits for 60 years or longer. The tree stands on the Moluccas thrives in the shade under groves of lofty trees. The nutmeg fruit is a pendulous drupe, similar in appearance to an apricot. When fully matured, it splits into two, exposing a crimson coloured aril, the mace, surrounding a single shiny brown seed, the nutmeg. The pulp of the fruit is eaten locally. After collection, the aril-enveloped nutmegs are conveyed to curing areas where the mace is removed, flattened out and dried. The nutmegs are dried slowly in the sun and turned twice daily over a period of 6 to 8 months. During this time, the nutmeg shrinks away from its hard seed coat until the kernels rattle in their shells when shaken. The shell is then broken with a wooden truncheon and the nutmegs are picked out. Dried nutmegs are greenish brown with furrowed surfaces. Large ones may be about 1.2 inch long and 0.8 inch in diameter.

The nutmeg and mace contain 7% to 14% essential oil, the principal components of which are pinene, camphene and dipentene. The oils are used as condiments and carminatives and to scent soaps and perfumes.

37. Asafoetida (Hing):

Botanically it is known as Ferula narthex Boisa. It is a gum-resin relished as a condiment in India and Iran where it is used to flavour curries, meatballs, dal and pickles. It has been used in Europe and the U.S. in perfumes and for flavouring. Acrid in taste, it emits a strong onion-like odour because of its organic sulphur compounds.

The whole plant is used as a fresh vegetable, the inner portion of the full grown stem being regarded as a luxury. The plant may grow as high as 7 ft. (2 metres). After 4 years, when it is ready to yield asafoetida, the stems are cut down close to the root and a milky juice flows out that quickly sets into a solid resinous mass. A freshly exposed surface of asafoetida has a translucent pearly white appearance, but it soon darkens in the air, becoming first pink and finally reddish brown.

The gum that exudes from the rootstock is commercially known as asafoetida; the raw gum is nauseous and so the fried gum is used for medicinal purposes. It is digestive, nervine, stimulant and expectorant. It is commonly used in flatulence, colic, dyspepsia, asthma, hysteria, convulsions, chronic bronchitis, cough and cold disorders of the bowels, epilepsy and angina pectoris. It should not be taken by a pregnant woman as it is a strong abortifacient.

38. Walnut (Akrot):

It is a deciduous tree of the genus Juglans family Juglandaceae, native to North and South America, southern Europe, Asia and the West Indies. Black walnut trees are valuable timber trees that produce edible nuts. A black walnut tree is about 30 metres tall and about 60 to 90 centimetres in diameter. With a deeply furrowed dark-brown or grayish black bark. The nut contains a sweet, oily seed and is enclosed in a yellow green hairy husk. The dark, fine-grained wood of English and black walnut is used for furniture, panelling and gunstocks. The fruit is very rich in vitamin C, it is very useful in heartburn, colic and dysentery. It removes impotency.

39. Olive (Jalpai):

It is a subtropical, broad-leafed, evergreen tree. The edible fruit is pressed to obtain olive oil. The trees ranging in height from 10 to 49 ft. or more has numerous branches; its leaves are leathery and lance shaped, dark-green above and silvery on the underside and are paired opposite each other on the twig. The wood is resistant to decay; if the top dries away, a new trunk will often arise from the roots. The tree's beauty has been extolled for thousands of years. The tree blooms in late spring, whitish flowers are borne in loose clusters in the axils of the leaves. Flowers are of two types, perfect, containing both male and female parts, which are capable of developing into the olive fruits; and male which contain only the pollen producing parts. The olive is wind-pollinated.

Olives are grown mainly for production of olive oil. Fresh, unprocessed olives are inedible because of their bitterness resulting from a glucoside that can be neutralised by treatment with a dilute alkali such as lye. Salt application also dispel some of the bitterness.

40. Isabgul:

Botanically it is know as Plantago ovata Forak. It is an almost stemless small herb, covered with dense or soft hairy growth. Leaves are 8 to 25 cm long and very narrow. Flowers are minute. Seeds are boat-shaped. The seeds of this plant constitute the drug. Isabgul is very useful in acute constipation and in dysentery both amoebic and bacillary. It is also useful as a soothing agent for mucous membranes. Isabgul is obtained by crushing the seeds and separating the husk by winnowing. The embryo oil of seeds having 50% linoleic acid prevents stroke.

41. Chick-pea or gram (Chhola or chana):

Botanically it is known as Cicer arietinum Linn. It is annual plant of the pea family native to Asia. It grows to about 2 feet tall and has a bushy appearance. The compound leaves are pinnate with alternate roundish, toothed leaflets. The small flowers are white or reddish and are followed by short pods containing one or two seeds. These are edible and resemble the garden pea.

Gram contains acids, amino acids, carotenoids, vitamins A, C and E and other constituents like niacin, lecithin, phytin, saponin, biochanin A, biochanin B and biochanin C. Several scientists at Dhaka University carried out research to find the medicinal properties of gram. They have found that during germination of the seed, more niacin is produced; consequently the juice is then more beneficial. Niacin is a vitamin mainly known and acclaimed for its ability to prevent pellagra, a disease which is characterised by gastro-intestinal disturbances and skin lesions, while vitamin C is necessary to fortify the body against infections and colds. Kernels of maize contain more niacin than do kernels of starchier varieties.

Medicinal uses of gram

Weakness and general debility: Soaked gram (germinated) is an age-old remedy in weakness, fatigue and general debility.

Fevers: The water in which the gram is boiled may be used in fevers for relief.

Urinary disorders: The water in which the gram is soaked is considered as very useful in urinary disorders.

Respiratory troubles: The water in which the gram is boiled may give some relief.

42. Apricot (Khobani):

It is a stone-fruit of the family Rosaceae, cultivated generally throughout the temperate regions of the world and used fresh for dessert or preserved by canning and drying. Trees are large and spreading with broad, heart shaped leaves. Dark green in colour and held erect on the twigs. The flowers are white in full bloom and borne singly or doubly at a node on very short stems. The apricot sets fruit often on self-pollination of its blossoms. The pit is smooth resembling that of plum but broader and more winged. The fruit is nearly smooth, round to oblong in some varieties, somewhat flattened and in general like peach in shape. Flesh is typically an attractive yellow to yellowish orange. The kernels of some varieties are sweet.

Native to China, the apricot is cultivated in all of central and south eastern Asia and in parts of southern Europe and north Africa. The leader in apricot production is Spain. Next comes in order are Iran, Syria, the U.S., France, Italy and Yugoslavia.

Apricots are good source of vitamin A and are high in natural sugar content. Dried apricots are excellent source of iron.

43. Currant (Karamcha, boch):

It is a shrub of the genus Ribes of the gooseberry family, the piquant, juicy berries of which are used chiefly in jams and jellies. There are at least 100 species. It is usually grown in England and America. Both red and black currants are used in lozenges for flavouring and are occasionally fermented.

Currants are very high in vitamin C and also supply calcium, phosphorus and iron. Great Britain ranks first in producing black currants which flourish best in cool, moist, and northern climates. Clay and silt soils are considered best.

44. Peach:

It is a fruit tree of the Rose family (Rosaceae) grown throughout the warmer temperate regions of both Northern and Southern hemisphere. The tree seldom reaches 21 ft in height; Under cultivation, it is usually kept between 10 to 13 ft by pruning. Leaves are glossy green, lance shaped and long pointed. The flowers borne in the leaf axils are arranged singly or in groups of two or three at nodes along with the shoots of the previous season's growth.

The peach develops from a single ovary that ripens into a fleshy, juicy exterior making up the edible part of the fruit and a hard interior called the stone or pit. The flesh my be white, yellow or red.

45. Pea-nut or groundnut (China-badam):

It is not a tree nut but the pod or legume of Arachis hypogaea which has the peculiar habit of ripening underground. It is a concentrated food. Peanuts have more protein, minerals and vitamins than beaf liver; more fat than heavy cream; and more calories than sugar.

The plant is an annual ranging from an erect or bunch form 450 to 600 millimetres (18 to 24 inches) high with short branches spreading to a runner that lies close to the soil. The stems and branches are sturdy and hairy; leaves are pinnately composed with two pairs of leaflets. The flowers are borne in the axils of the leaves. The peanut is grown mainly for its edible oil (badam tel) except in the U.S. where it is produced for grinding into peanut butter, for roasted salted nuts and for use in candy and bakery products. A small percentage of the U.S. crop is crushed for oil. The tops of the plants after the pods are removed are fed as hay.

Peanut is very effective in curing impotency. It gives sexual vigour and sexual strength.

46. Quince:

It is a fruit of the genus Cydonia of the Rose family (Rosaceae). The much branched small trees have entire leaves with small stipules and bear large, solitary white or pink flowers like those of the pear or apple but with leafy calyx lobes and a many-celled ovary, in each cell of which are numerous horizontal ovules. The fruits may be round and flattened or somewhat pear-shaped.

The common quince is usually grown in Iran, Turkey, Greece and Crimea. The Japanese quince has been widely used as an ornamental shrub in gardens particularly before the leaves open fully in late winter and early spring. Some of the small shrubs bear large, green, fragrant fruits that are inedible in the fresh state but have been used in making preserves.

The fruits are golden yellow in colour and the flesh takes on a pink colour when cooked giving an attractive colour to jellies and conserves. The fruit has a strong aroma and in the raw state is astringent but it makes excellent preserves and is often used to give flavour and sharpness to stewed or baked apples.

47. Custard apple (Ata or nona):

The fruit of the common custard apple or bullock's heart of the West Indies is dark brown in colour and marked with depressions giving it a quilted appearance; its pulp is reddish yellow, sweetish and very soft; the kernels of the seeds are said to be poisonous. The sour-sop is produced in West Indies. The sweet-sop is grown in Tropical America. Alligator-apple or cork-wood is grown in South America and West Indies which is favoured for its wood. This wood is used as cork. The fruit alligator-apple is not eaten fresh but is sometimes used for making jellies.

48. Sugarcane (Akh):

A giant perennial grass of the genus Saccharum native to the tropical and sub-tropical zones. The plant includes chumps of solid stalks with regularly shaped joints or nodes at each of which occurs a single bud or eye. The graceful sword-shaped leaves are similar to those of corn and the leaf sheath folds around the stem, protecting the bud. Mature canes may be 10 to 26 ft. tall and are usually 1/2 to 2 inches in diameter; the dimensions vary with local conditions, length of growing period and variety of cane. The colour of the cane ranges from almost white to yellow to deep green, purple red or violet. Some varieties have striped or ribbon canes of variegated colours.

It is grown primarily in South and Central America, Africa and Asia. The largest grower of sugarcane is India. Next comes Java.

Sugarcane consists of 20% sucrose, 4% to 13% ash, nil to 2% invert sugar, 8% to 16% fibre and 70% to 75% water. The fibre essentially cellulose and related materials represent the bulk of the insoluble portion of the cane and it is used as bagasse after the extraction of sugar. The chief bye-products of the sugar industry are bagasse, gur, khandsari, molasses and aconitic acid.

The sugarcane juice is a tonic, rejuvenative and refreshing drink during hot summer months. It subsides pitta. It prevents sun-stroke, heat-stroke and keeps the body cool and calm. It removes constipation. It is very useful in jaundice.

49. Pea (Matar):

Botanically it is known as Pisum sativum. It is the common name for several species of herbaceous annuals of the family Fabaceae grown for edible seeds, borne in pods or legumes. The stems of the pea plant are hollow and climbing. Leaves are pinnately compound, ending in tendrils that enable the plant to climb. The flowers are butterfly-like in shape and are coloured white or purple. The fruit is one-celled, many seeded pod, which splits into halves when ripe; the 5 to 10 seeds are attached by short stalks to the halves of the pod. Some varieties called sugar-peas produce edible pods that are popular in the Orient. Dried peas are sometimes ground to make flour.

Green peas consist of water 74.3%, protein 6.7%, fat 94%, ash 0.9%, fibre 2.2%, sugar 3.2%, starch 8.2% and other carbohydrates 4.1%. Measurable amounts of vitamins A, B and C are found in fresh green peas. Green peas are very useful in weakness, general debility, anaemia, and in run-down conditions. It is called 'poor man's egg'.

50. Liquorice (Jastimadhu):

Botanically it is called Glycyrrhiza glabra. It is a tall erect herb that may rise up to 1.5 m high. Leaves are compound containing leaflets in 4 to 7 pairs. The flowers are like lilac, small. the fruits are 1.3 cm long, flat, densely covered all over with small spinous outgrowths. The rootstock gives numerous additional roots. The plant is grown in Kashmir, Dehra Dun, Delhi etc.

The dried roots and underground stems of this plant constitute the drug. Liquorice is a house-hold remedy for coughs and cold, bronchitis, fevers, abdominal pains, consumption and epilepsy. It is also given in urinary and kidney disorders. The powder or small pieces of the drug are commonly taken with betel leaves. Liquorice is largely used in making syrup. It is also useful in gastric or peptic ulcers.

51. Dandelion:

It is a weedy perennial herb of the genus Taraxacum of the family Asterceae, widely grown in Eurasia but also produced in North America. It has a rosette of leaves at the base of the plant; a deep taproot; a smooth hollow stem; leaves are smooth-margined, toothed or deeply cut; and a solitary yellow flower. The fruit is a ball-shaped cluster of many small, tufted one-seeded fruits. The bitter young leaves are used in salads and the roots can be used to make a coffee-like beverage.

52. Collard:

It is a form of cabbage of the mustard family (Brassicaceae). Collard leaves are much broader and are not frilled and resemble rosette leaves of hard cabbage. The main stem reaches a height of 24 to 48 inches with a rosette of leaves at the top. The entire young rosette is sometimes harvested. The plant is a source of vitamins A and C. It is widely adapted, easily grown and quite commonly raised as a source of winter greens in the southern United States.

53. Celery:

It is a herb of the family Apiaceae usually grown in the Medeterranean areas. Celery fruit was used as a flavouring agent by the ancient Greeks and Romans and as medicine by the ancient Chinese. Celery fruits are very small, rarely more than 1 inch in size; they are grey brown in colour. The aroma of celery seed is that of the vegetable; the taste is that of celery, warm and slightly bitter. It is used to flavour foods, particularly soups and pickles. The fruit juice is given in asthma, bronchitis, spleen disorders, urinary troubles and rheumatism.

54. Avocado:

It is a fruit of Persea americana of the family Lauraceae usually grown in the Western Hemisphere from Mexico south to the Andean regions. The tree, tall and spreading, has leaves elliptic to egg-shaped in form and 4 to 12 inches in length. The small greenish flowers born in dense racemes are devoid of petals and have six perianth lobes, nine stamens arranged on three series, a one-celled ovary. The fruit is exceedingly variable in shape, size and colour. It looks like hen's egg and it varies from round to pear shaped with a long slender neck. The colour ranges from green to dark purple. The single large seed with two cotyledons is round to conical.

Horticulturally, avocados are divided into Mexican, West Indian and Guatemala races. The Mexican variety is characterised by the anise-like odour of the leaves and thin skinned fruits of rich flavour and excellent quality. The Guatemalan type is slightly less frost resistant than the Mexican and produces fruit of medium to large size. West Indian type is grown in southern Florida.

55. Brazil nut:

It is also known as paranut, butter-nut, cream-nut castanea and niygertoe. It is an edible fruit of a large South American tree Bertholetia excelsa (family Lecythidaceae). The globular fruit about 2 to 4 inches in diameter and hard-walled contains 8 to 24 nuts or seeds arranged like sections of an orange. The harvest period is from January to June. The tree is of great value for timber which is not hardy but very light.

Brazil nuts are high in fat and contain protein, iron and thiamine.

56. Bread fruit:

It is a fruit of a tree belonging to the family Morceal which is grown only in the South Pacific region (Malay). It is a staple food there. The tree grows from 40 to 60 ft high and has large oval, glossy green leaves three to nine lobed toward the apex. Male and female flowers are borne in separate groups of flowers on the same tree. The ripe fruits or matured ovaries of these pistillate flowers are roundish, 4 to 8 inches in diameter, greenish to brownish green and have a white somewhat fibrous pulp.

57. Plum (Kul):

It is a fruit of the genus Prunus of the rose family (Rosaceae). Like peach and cherry, it is a stone or drupe fruit. The tree reaches a height of from 20 to 33 ft. The flower buds of most varieties are borne on short spurs or along the terminal shoots of the main branches. Each bud may contain one to 5 flowers. As the fruit grows, the outer part of the ovary ripens into a fleshy juicy exterior making up the edible part of the fruit and a hard interior called the stone or pit. The seed is enclosed within the stone. The fruits show a wide range of size, flavour, colour and tincture. A liquor called sijivovica made from plums is an important article of commerce in Yugoslavia. The fruit relieves nausea and checks purging.

58. Mango (Aam):

Botanically it is known as Mangifera indica. It is a member of the cashew family (Anacardiacea), one of the most important and widely cultivated fruits of the tropical world. The tree is evergreen, often reaching 50 to 60 ft in height and attaining great age. Leaves are lanceolate, up to 12 inches long; the flowers small, pinkish and fragrant, are borne in large terminal panicles.

The fruit varies greatly in size and character; the smallest mangoes are no larger than plums, while others may weigh 4 to 5 pds. Its form is oval, round, heart shaped, kidney shaped or long and slender. Some varieties are beautifully coloured with shades of red and yellow, while others are dull green. The single large seed is flattened, the flesh that surrounds it is yellow to orange in colour, juicy, sweet and of delicious spicy flavour. Mangoes are a rich source of vitamins A, C and D.

The unripe fruit is acidic, astringent and antiscorbutic; the ripe fruit is antiscorbutic, diuretic, laxative, invigorating, fattening, and astringent. Sun dried slices of the unripe fruit is very useful in scurvy. The fried skin of the unripe fruit is given with sugar in menorrhagia. The fruit juice increases sexual vigour and sexual strength. It cures impotency. The ripe fruit is often used as a sexual tonic.

59. Toddy palm (Tal):

Its botanical name is Borassus fiabelliter Linn. The palm tree is extensively cultivated in India for its fresh sweetish juice. The juice of the fresh fruit is refrigerant. The fresh sweetish juice flowing from cuts made on the flowering stalk is cooling, stimulant, antiphlegmatic and antiphlogistic. If taken regularly, it acts as a laxative. It is given in dropsy, inflammatory affections and gastric catarrh. The slightly fermented juice is given in diabetes, and with aromatics in phthisis. Palm-sugar prepared from toddy is used as a antidote in poisoning; as it is antibilious, it is given in liver troubles and gleet.

60. Wood-apple (Kathbel):

Botanically it is called Feronica limorria Swingle. The unripe fruit is astringent and is administered in diarrhoea and dysentery. The ripe fruit is refreshing, aromatic, antiscorbutic, carminative, digestive, tonic and antidotal. It is often used as a stomachic.

61. Hog-plum (Amra):

Its botanical name is Spondias mombin. It is also called yellow mombin, ornamental purplish green flowered tree of the cashew family (Anacardiaceae), native to tropical areas of the world. The hog plum are cultivated for its edible fruits called ciuela. The large stone in each fruit bears many spines and is difficult to separate from the pulp. The ripe fruit is chiefly used in salads and pickles. It is stomachic. It subsides pitta. The fruit juice is cooling and refreshing. It prevents sun-stroke, heat-stroke, vomiting and travel sickness.

62. Loquat:

It is a sub-tropical tree of the rose family (Rosaceae) related to the apple. Ornamental in appearance and rarely more than 33 ft in height, the evergreen loquat is frequently planted in parks and gardens. The leaves, clustered toward the ends of branches are thick and stiff, elliptic to lanceolate, from 8 to 10 inches in length with closely serrate margins. The fruits are borne in large, loose clusters, individually. They are round, or pear-shaped, 1 to 3 inches in length with a tough yellow to bronze, plum-like skin enclosing juicy, whitish to orange coloured flesh surrounding 3 to 4 large seeds. The flavour is agreeably tart. In Japan it was much developed horticulturally and is still highly valued.

63. Jack-fruit (Kanthal, inchar):

Botanically, it is called Artocarpus heterophylla. It is an attractive tropical tree valued for its immense fruits and its timber. It grows to 60 ft high and bears variable shaped evergreen leaves. The Jack-fruit, a member of the mulberry family (Moraceae), is native to eastern India and is extensively grown in tropical Asia. It has also been widely introduced into the American tropics.

Its fruit resembles bread-fruit but are of inferior quality. It is a staple food of tropical Asia. Jack-fruits are 12 to 20 inches long and 8 to 10 inches thick and commonly weigh 18 kg or more. The pulp of the ripe fruit is eaten raw. Green fruits are very nutritious vegetable which is called inchar and is usually eaten in soups and stews. The ripe fruit is not very good for health as it may cause diarrhoea and even cholera. The ripe fruit is very dangerous and should not be taken more than 3 to 4 bulbs at a time during summer months. Its wood is valued for cabinet work.

64. Black-berry (Kalajam):

Botanically it is known as Polianthes tuberosa. It is a large tree 20 to 60 ft. high or sometimes more. The leaves are elliptical, usually 6 to 12 inches long. The fruits are black containing juicy, fleshy rind and are delicious and nutritious too. It is one-seeded fruit and the seed is usually a large one. The tree is extensively cultivated all over India for its fruits.

Black-berries are available only during summer months. The fruit juice is valuable in summer time as it subsides bile (pitta). It presents sun-stroke, heat-stroke and keeps the body cool. It has special qualities to stop vomiting and travel sickness.

Medicinal uses of black-berry :

The bark, fruits and seeds of the tree are medicinal. The bark is very astringent and is given in sore throat, bronchitis, asthma, ulcers and dysentery; it is also used for purifying blood. The fresh juice of the bark with goat's milk is given in diarrhoea. The seeds are very useful in diabetes. The fruit juice cures burning sensation of hands and feet. It subsides excessive heat in the body.

65. Nectarine:

It is smooth-skinned peach which may be obtained from the seed of a peach or from peach by bud mutation. The smooth skin of the nectarine behaves as a recessive character to the pubescence of the peach. When the pubescent character is homozygous, all peach and a nectarine will be peaches; while if the peach is heterozygous for skin covering, the resulting progeny segregate in the ratio of one peach to one nectarine. The nectarine possesses a distinctive pleasing flavour and the tree and fruit characteristics of the peach. Nectarine is usually grown in California and it succeeds where the peach is grown. It will become more popular with the advent of superior varieties and better control methods against insects and diseases. Nectarine is a rich source of vitamins A and C. It also contains minerals. This fruit is very useful in cases of bronchitis, anaemia, scurvy, rickets, low vitality and general debility.

66. Nasturtium:

It is a plant of the genus Tropaeolum, usually grown for their orange, yellow or red flowers. The common garden nasturtium is an annual that has given rise to many varieties differing in stature and in colour or flavour. The leaves and flowers of this plant can be eaten in salads and the young fruits can be picked and used like capers. It is cultivated in Andean Highlands for its tubers that are used for food. It contains vitamins and minerals. It is very delicious and nutritious.

67. Kumquat:

It is a citrus fruit looking like small orange. Four species are known, all originating in China and Japan. Kumquats reach maximum height of about 5 ft. They have pointed elliptical leaves; small white, star-shaped flower, and sometimes thorns. The orange coloured fruit is usually round to oblong and often less than 2 inches in length. It has a sweet or acid taste and may be eaten raw or as marmalade. Kumquats are also ornamentals. Kumquats are very rich in vitamins A, B and C. It also contains minerals. This fruit is very useful in bronchitis, cough and cold, laryngitis, pharyngitis, sore throat, fevers, diarrhoea, dysentery, spleen disorders etc.

68. Mandarin & Tangerine:

These are small oranges with light peel.

THE VEGETABLES

69. Spinach (Palang sak):

Botanically it is called Spinacia oleracea of the Goosefoot family (Chemopocliaceae), a leafy annual used as a vegetable. The edible leaves are arranged in a rosette from which a seedstock subsequently emerges. The leaves are somewhat triangular and may be flat or puckered. Spinach requires cool weather and deep, rich, well-lined soil to give quick growth and maximum leaf area. Seeds can be sown every two weeks in early winter in rows 12 inches apart; the plantlets being thinned in a row. The last sowing produces young plants that yield a crop.

Widely grown in Northern U.S., India and other parts of the world, spinach is marketed fresh, canned and frozen. It has a high content of iron, vitamins A, B, C, E, and K. Spinach is served as salad green and as a cooked vegetable. In classical cuisine, spinach is made into various soups, souffles and mousses and is used as an ingredient in various prepared dishes.

The fresh leaves are an excellent source of vitamin C, iron, calcium and phosphorus. As such, the leaves are valuable in cases of pernicious anaemia, low vitality, sterility, impotency, neuralgia, tired nerves and nervous debility. It is a nervine tonic.

Spinach is good for those who are in need of iron, taking spinach leaf juice either raw or by cooking as stew or soups. Spinach leaf juice is good for sore throat to be used as gargle. It is specially useful for pregnant women who need large amount of iron for health of the baby inside. You will find that doctors usually prescribe ferrous sulphate (iron salt) in time of pregnancy.

'The natural system for curing disease is based on a return to Nature in regulating the diet, breathing, exercising, bathing and the employment of various other natural forces to eliminate the poisonous substances in the system and so raise the vitality and health of the patient'.—Dr. John B. Lust.

70. Cabbage (Bandhakapi):

Botanically it is called Brassica oleracea. It is a biennial vegetable and foddar plant. It is cultivated near the sea coast of various parts of England, in India and the U.S. This plant grows best in mild to cool climate, tolerate frost and some of them tolerate hard freezing at certain points of growth. Hot weather impairs the growth and quality of them. Edible portion of these plants are low in calorie value.

Head cabbage is by far the most important form. Hard-headed cabbage is a newcrop plant that was developed in northern Europe during the middle ages. Soft headed cabbage such as Savoy type is believed to be of southern European origin of an earlier time. Head cabbage is generally denoted by the simple term cabbage and is a major table vegetable in most countries of the temperate zones. The head cabbage ranges in shape from pointed through globular to flat; from soft to hard in structure; though various shades of green grey, magenta or red, and from less than 1 kg to more than 5 kg in weight.

It is an excellent source of vitamin C, iron and calcium. It is valuable in cases of afternoon headache, listlessness, sighing, brooding, fear, pessimism, heart palpitation, neuralgia, bronchitis, jaundice and trembling.

The use of cabbage juice for treatment of stomach ulcers is one of the latest and most vital advances in the field of juice therapy. The healing agent, vitamin U, was isolated and identified by Dr. Garnett Cheney of the Stanford University of Medicine. The treatment consisted of the addition of a quart of cabbage juice to the daily diet taken 5 times a day in six ounce quantities. Cabbage juice should be taken in raw state and without the addition of salt.

The anti-ulcer factor vitamin U is destroyed by cooking. Therefore in the tests made by Dr. Garnett Cheney with gastric ulcer patients, no other raw food was permitted. This proved that fresh cabbage juice alone, transmitted the healing units of vitamin U. The therapeutic effect of the treatment was shown periodically by X-ray examination.

Dr. Garnett Cheney has opined that one-half pint of raw cabbage juice, properly prepared, contains more organic food value than does two hundred pounds of cooked or canned cabbage.

Dr. Benedict Lust has opined that raw cabbage juice added to carrot juice forms an excellent source of vitamin C as a cleansing medium, particularly where infection of the gums with resultant pyorrhoea is present.

71. Cauliflower (Phulkapi):

Botanically cauliflower is known as Brassica oleracea. It is a form of cabbage of the mustard family (Brassicaceae), consists of a compact terminal mass of greatly thickened, modified and partially developed flower structure, together with their fleshy stalks.

As desired for food, this terminal cluster forms a firm, white, succulent 'curd'. The broad, much-elongated leaves extend far above this curd. In most varieties, the leaves must be tied together well above the curd or broken over it several days before harvest to prevent discolouration of the curd by sunlight.

Cauliflower is frequently served as cooked vegetable and the separated flower structures are also used in salads and as relishes in raw form.

Cauliflower is a rich source of vitamins, iron and other minerals. It contains vitamins A, B and C. For juice purposes, cauliflower is not so useful. It is usually eaten as cooked or boiled, in soups, curries and stews.

72. Egg-plant (Brinjal, Baigon):

Botanically it is known as Solanum melongena. It is a tender perennial plant of the nightshade family (Solanaceae) closely allied to the potato. Egg-plant requires a warm climate and is grown extensively in eastern and southern Asia and in the United States. It has an erect, bushy stem sometimes armed with a few spikes; large, ovate, slightly lobed leaves and pendant; violet, usually solitary flowers about 2 inches across. The fruit is a large, egg-shaped berry, varying in colour from dark purple to violet, yellowish or white. It his sometimes ridged, and has a shining surface. It is served as a baked, grilled, fried, boiled or roasted vegetable and is used as garnish in stews and soups.

Brinjal contains vitamins A, B and C and iron in plenty. For juice purposes, this vegetable is not used.

73. Plantain (Kanchkala):

Botanically it is known as Musa paradisiaca. It is a plant of the banana family (Musaceae) closely related to the common banana (Musa sapientum). The plant is 10 to 33 ft. high with large fleshy tree-like stems having bright green leaves. The fruit which is green is larger than banana. The edible fruit of the plant has more starch than the banana and is not eaten raw. It is usually cooked green either boiled or fried with coconut juice or sugar as a flavouring. It may also be dried for later use in cooking or ground for use as a meal. The meal can be further refined to flour. Plantain is now an export crop of India. In East Africa, it is a staple food and beer-making crop, specially in Uganda and Tanzania.

This plant originated in India. Later it was introduced in other tropical regions like Africa, Egypt, America and Indonesia. There are two types of plantain, viz. the horn plantain and the French plantain.

For juice purposes plantain is not used. But plantain flower (mocha) juice is very useful in menorrhagia. Plantain is a rich source of vitamin A, B and O. It also contains other minerals.

74. Beans (Sim):

It is a seed or pod of certain leguminous plants of the family Fabaceae originally of Vicia faba, an old world species called Windsor bean, broad bean, mung bean and horse-bean. The mature seeds of the principal beans used, except soyabean, are rather similar in composition, although they differ widely in taste. Beans are used for cooking either fresh or dried.

It is a climbing plant 50 to 80 inches long. Dwarf and semi-climbers are grown extensively. When the climbing type is grown for its immature pods, artificial props are necessary to facilitate harvesting. Varieties differ greatly in size, shape, colour and fibrousness or tenderness of the immature pods.

Most edible podded beans produce relatively low yields of mature seeds. Seed colours range from white through green, yellow, tan, pink, red, brown and purple to black in solid colours and countless controlling patterns.

The mung bean is widely cultivated in India. The pods and seeds are by far the smallest of any of the beans named here. The pods are slender, 3 to 4 inches long and contain 10 to 14 spherical to oblong seeds.

The horsegram and the bhavist bean native to India are relatively large tropical climbing plants, the immature seeds of which are used for food in Asia. The dry seeds are large, dark to black, nearly round to slightly flattened and elongated.

The bean is very rich in iron and so useful in time of pregnancy. It also contains vitamins A, B and C. Bean is usually eaten as a cooked vegetable.

75. Chilli or red pepper (Mircha, Kanchalanka):

Botanically, it is Capsicum frutescens. It is also known as chilli pepper or green pepper. Usually very small, very hotly pungent fruits of Capsicum plants are used to make chilli powder and to flavour barbecue, hot curry and other spicy sauces. Chillis are used in medicine to stimulate the flow of gastric juices. The pungent principle of Capsicum is capsicin, a substance with a burning taste and very acrid vapours.

Chillis are cultivated in Equatorial Africa, India, Japan, Mexico, and the U.S. It is a shrubby perennial 6 to 8 feet high with small whitish flowers. It is capable of bearing fruits in the first year. The chilli pepper bears long, tapering, usually pungent red or yellow fruits 4 to 10 inches in length. Dried chilli peppers are ground to make cayenne pepper or red pepper for seasoning. Chillis are eaten cooked or as spices.

76. Holy basil or Sacred basil (Tulsi or tulasi) :

Botanically it is known as Ocimum sanctum Linn. It is an erect, soft, hairy herb. The leaves are ovate or elliptic-oblong. The tree is widely grown in

India and Pakistan. The leaves are expectorant, stomachic, anticatarrhal, diaphoretic and aromatic; their decoction is given in malaria, gastric diseases of children and liver disorders. As a prophylactic against malaria, fresh leaves are eaten with black-pepper in the morning. The leaf juice with honey is a household remedy for chronic fever and dyspepsia. The leaf juice is locally applied for ringworm and other skin diseases and for relief of earache.

A decoction of the roots is also very useful in malarial fever. A paste of the fresh roots is applied to bites of insects and leeches. The leaf juice with honey and liquorice is an age-old remedy for cough and cold.

77. Pumpkin (Lau):

Botanically it is known as Cucurbita maxima. The quick-growing, small-fruited bush or non-trailing varieties of C. pepo are called squash in America, while the long-season, long-trailing, large-fruited varieties are called pumpkin in India or other tropical countries.

The fruits are large, generally 4 to 8 kg in weight; usually white, oblong, round or elongated in shape. The largest variety may weigh 30 kg or more. Pumpkins are commonly grown in North America, Great Britain, Europe and India, for human food and also for livestock feed. The rind is removed and the pulp is cooked. The seeds are small, white and flat and lie in rows within the fruit. The fruit and seeds are used for medicinal purposes. The fruit juice is often applied as beauty aid.

Pumpkins contain vitamins A, B, C and G and minerals. Pumpkin juice is very useful in cases of sun-stroke, heat-stroke, acidity, and liver troubles. It keeps the body cool during hot summer months.

The medicinal uses of pumpkin seeds and fruits are enumerated as under:

Beauty aid: Pumpkin juice is often applied externally on the face to remove dirt, black spots, and to make the skin soft and lovely.

Cataract: Pumpkin juice with water is very useful in case of cataract. It is to be applied locally.

Leucoderma: White patches on the skin can be easily removed by applying pumpkin flower juice several times daily.

Pyorrhoea: This disease can be cured by gargling with roasted pumpkin juice.

Acidity: Roasted pumpkin juice is a household remedy for acidity.

Piles: The fruit juice is very useful in piles and fistula.

Prostate gland disorders or urinary troubles: Pumpkin seeds are usually prescribed in prostate gland disorders.

Tapeworm: Pumpkin seeds are very useful in removing tapeworm.

Impotency and sterility: Pumpkin fruits offer an inexhaustible source of vigour and vitality to the body. They are very rich in phosphorus, iron, vitamin A and B, calcium, protein and fat. They have some nutritional effects on male sex organs and thereby makes them strong and healthy. They are very good in case of impotency or sterility.

78. Horse-radish/Ben oil tree (Sajne danta):

Botanically it is known as Moringa oleifera Lan. It is popularly called as 'Sovanjan'. The fruits contain iron, vitamin A and C, calcium, riboflavin, protein and carbohydrates. They are stimulant, diuretic and antiasthmatic. The leaf, flowers, fruit, seed, bark, root and gum are used for medicinal purposes. This plant possesses anti-biotic properties. The fruit is generally used as small-pox vaccine.

The leaves are very useful in scurvy and catarrhal diseases. A poultice of the leaves is often applied to wounds, boils and swellings. The bark of the stem is a cardiac stimulant and used in asthma, cough and cold. It is also used locally as a counter-irritant in rheumatism and nervous pains. A hot decoction of the root-bark is used to relieve earache, and in dental cavities to remove toothache. A powder of the root-bark is often used as snuff in cases of headache, earache and toothache.

Several medical books and ayurvedic texts have described the various medicinal uses of horse-radish.

Fruit and Vegetable Juice Therapy 119

These are enumerated as under:

Leaf: Leaf juice is often used to reduce high blood pressure. The tender leaves are given in scurvy and catarrhal diseases. A poultice of fresh leaves is applied to wounds, boils and swellings.

Flowers: Flowers are eaten as vegetables in order to prevent the possible attack of small-pox in spring. They are also very useful in asthma, bronchitis, cough and cold, spleen and liver troubles.

Root: The fresh root of a young tree is valuable in intermittent fever, epilepsy, hysteria, palsy, chronic rheumatism, gout, dropsy, dyspepsia and enlargement of liver and spleen.

Fruit (Sajne danta): It contains iron, amino acids, proteins, and vitamins A, B and C in plenty. The raw fruit is very helpful in rheumatism, arthritis, paralysis, smallpox, chicken-pox, toothache, and earache. It is prized as anti-pox vaccine.

Bark: Externally the bark juice is applied as paste in ringworm.

Ben oil: It is rubbed locally on the painful joints of rheumatic and gouty patients. This offers great relief.

Seeds: The seeds are valuable in cases of venereal diseases and ascites.

Gum: The gum that exudes from the stem is taken with milk for relief of headache; it is locally applied on the forehead. The fried gum is eaten for relief of windiness. The gum is an efficacious drink for glandular swellings. The gum mixed with mustard oil is very useful in toothache and earache.

79. White pumpkin (Chal-kumro):

Botanically white pumpkin is known as Benincasa hispida. More popularly it is called Kashunda. It is a herbaceous climbing plant, for which artificial supports are necessary for its proper growth. It is extensively cultivated in India, particularly in Bengal. The fruit is oval through round and elliptical in shape. Its weight varies from 1 kg to 8 kg or more.

The fruit contains vitamin B1 and fatty oil. It is tonic, digestive, stomachic, and a mild laxative. The raw fruit is very useful in inflammation of the heart and lungs. This is also given in pleurisy, consumption, worms, flatulence and urinary disorders. It is also used as a tonic for the brain and stomach.

Several medical books and ayurvedic texts have described the medicinal uses of white pumpkin as under:-

1. **Blood-vomiting:** The juice of the ripe fruit with sugar is an age-old remedy in blood-vomiting.

2. **Pleurisy:** Its juice with sugar offers great relief in pleurisy.

3. **Enlargement of heart and lungs:** Its juice

with milk offers and excellent remedy in enlargement of the heart and lungs.

4. **Urinary disorders:** Its juice constitutes a valuable remedy in urinary disorders.

5. **Excessive sex urge:** Its juice keeps the excessive sex urge under control.

6. **Flatulence:** It is often used as a stomachic.

7. **Brain disorders:** Its juice keeps he brain calm and cool.

80. Endive:

Endive is an edible annual leafy plant of the family Asteraceae, variably believed to have originated in Egypt and Indonesia and cultivated in Europe since the 16th century. Its many varieties form two groups, the much curled or narrow leaved and the Batavian or broad leaved as a biennial. About 3 months after sowing, the plants' outer leaves are tied together or are covered to exclude light. This prevents the development of the natural bitter taste. This bleaching process takes 10 days to 4 weeks.

Endive contains sufficient amount of vitamins A, B and C. This plant is not cultivated in India. Endive juice along with carrot and celery is very rich in vital minerals, i.e. iron, sodium and calcium. This is excellent in cases of asthma, skin diseases, biliousness, poor blood, gall-stones and gall-bladder irritation, diseases of the urinary tract, stomach ulcers, inflammation of middle ear and for general body building.

81. Acorn:

It is a fruit of the oak tree which is composed of a nut and a cup or involucre. The nut develops from the ovary of the female flower. The young ovary normally has three carpels each of which bears two or three ovules. Only one of the ovules ripens into a nut; the others abort and remain associated with the integument of the functional ovule. Thus the mature nut is celled and one-seeded. The acorn cup varies in different species from a deep cup-shaped to a shallow saucer-shaped structure formed by the hardened scales of the involucre.

The edible acorns of several species are used as food for human beings, especially in Asia. Lumber of oak trees is used for furniture, building and flooring. The bark is the source of cork used for sealing containers and insulation purposes. The insect galls on leaves of oak trees are used in ink manufacture and the leaves of several Asian species are used to rear silk-worms.

82. Artichoke:

Artichoke is a tall perennial plant widely cultivated in the mediterranean region and the Canary Islands. It is a coarse, stout, thistle-like herb, usually 3 to 5 ft tall. It has spiny-feathery leaves, the lower ones often 3 feet or more long. The flowers are usually blue or white.

Artichokes are extensively grown in southern Europe and the United States for their edible thickened scales and bottoms or hearts of the immature flowerheads. The common artichoke is sometimes called the Globe-artichoke or French-artichoke. A perennial American sunflower is often called the Jerusalem artichoke, although it is not an artichoke. The tuber of this plant is used as a vegetable in America. Artichokes are rich in iron, iodine, potassium and vitamins A and C. For juice purposes, it is rarely used.

83. Parsley:

It is a much branched bright green, smooth, biennial herb with ternately pinnate decompound crisped leaves, greenish yellow flowers in compound umbel, belonging to a small genus of the mediterranean plant of the parsley family Umbelliferae. Cultivated since antiquity, parsley is grown in a variety of forms. Seeding should be started early in spring either in the open or in a hot bed. As the seed germinates slowly, raddish seed may be planted along with it to make it sprout quickly.

Parsley is one of the commonest plants used in garnishing fish and meats or as an ingredient for stuffing fowl. The pleasant, mildly aromatic flavour makes appetising fish, meats, soups, sauces and salads. The leaves are usually gathered fresh and used as soon as possible.

Parsley contains less than 0.5% essential oil, the principal component of which is the pungent, oily, green liquid apiol. Turnip rooted parsley is grown for its large white parsnip-like root popular in Europe. Parsley leaves were used by the Romans and Greeks to flavour and garnish foods.

Parsley is a rich source of vitamin A and also C. Parsley juice should not be taken in quantities more than two ounces at a time, unless mixed with carrot or beet juice. It helps to maintain the blood vessels, particularly the capillaries and arterioles, in a healthy condition. Being an excellent food for the genito-urinary tract, it is very valuable in cases of bladder disorders, nephritis, albuminuria, and other kidney troubles.

Raw parsley juice mixed with carrot juice is very effective in every ailment connected with the eyes and optic nerves and will benefit weak eyes, ulceration of the cornea, cataract, conjunctivitis, ophthalmia or haziness of the pupil. Its juice should not be taken singly as it is very strong. It should be mixed with carrot or orange or musumbi juice.

84. Peppermint:

It is a strongly aromatic perennial herb providing a widely used flavouring. It has stalked, smooth, dark-green leaves and oblong-obtuse, spike-like clusters of pinkish lavender flowers which are dried and used to flavour candy desserts, beverages, salads, and other foods. Peppermint has a strong, agreeable, sweetish odour and a warm pungent taste with a cool aftertaste. Indigenous to Europe and Asia, it has since been naturalised in North America and is found near streams and at other wet sites. It is extensively cultivated for its essential oil.

Peppermint oil, a volatile oil distilled with steam from the herb, is widely used for flavouring confectionery, chewing gum, dentrifices and medicines. Pure oil of peppermint is nearly colourless. It consists primarily of menthol and menthane. Menthol is also called mint camphor and long used medicinally as a soothing balm all over the world. Peppermint oil is very useful in flatulence, nausea, gastralgia, and travel-sickness.

85. Parsnip:

It is member of the carrot family Apiaceae, cultivated since ancient times for its edible large tapering fleshy white root with a distinct flavour. The root is found in roadsides and open places in England and throughout Europe and temperate Asia.

Parsnip seed is sown in spring in rows about half metre apart and the plants thinned to stand 5 to 7 centimetres apart in the row. At the end of summer, the solids of the root consist largely of starch, but a period of low temperature changes much of the starch to sugar. The root is hardy and not damaged by hard freezing over the soil. The root has sweet flavour and is usually served as cooked vegetable. This plant is rarely used in raw juice therapy. Parsnip contains vitamin B1 and C.

86. Rhubarb/Pie plant:

Botanically it is known as Rheum rhaponticum. It is a perennial plant cultivated for its juicy acid leafstalks which are used for making pies, sauces, wine and preserves. It was originally grown in western Asia and later introduced in other parts of the world. Rhubarb has large leaves which have thick, fleshy stalks and it has small greenish white flowers. It is usually propagated by means of division of the roots, although seeds are also used. Rhubarb thrives best in rich, light, friable, loamy soils well-drained but moist. It responds to liberal application of manure in the fall. Harvest of stalks, may begin when the plants are two years old and the stalks should be pulled and not cut. Roots of Rhubarb should be divided every 3 to 4 years. The drug called Rhubarb, used mainly as a laxative, consists of dried roots and rhizomes of R. palmatum and R. officinale.

87. Chive:

It is a perennial onion-like plant whose pungent grass- like leaves are commonly used for flavouring salads, soups, cheese and omelettes. The chive, known technically as Allium schoenopram, belongs to the Amaryllis family (Amarylidaceae). It grows in thick tufts and produces small oval bulbs. Its small purplish flowers are borne in clusters but they produce few seeds. Consequently the plant is propagated by division of tufts. The chive is usually cultivated in Europe. In the United States, it is cultivated to a limited extent. It is not grown in India.

In commercial plantings, the chive is harvested divided into clumps which are placed in small clay pots and the old leaves are cut off. When new leaves form, the pots are crated and marketed. The consumer then grows the plant at home, cutting off leaves as needed. The chive is a rich source of vitamin C and minerals.

88. Chervil:

It is a name commonly applied to two plants of the parsley family both of which are cultivated for food. The salad chervil (Anthriscus cerefolium) has leaves that are similar in taste and appearance to those of parsley. They are used as a salad green, a garnish and as a seasoning in meat, loaf, soup and other dishes. They are also used to flavour vinegar. The salad chervil is generally cultivated in the Caucasus region of Russia, but has now become naturalised from Quebec to the United States. It is not grown in India.

The turnip root chervil is a biennial European plant grown for its edible carrot shaped roots which are grey on the outside and yellowish white inside. They are mostly eaten in stews or as a boiled or fried vegetable. Chervil contains iodine, potassium, fluorine and sulphur.

89. Chestnut:

Chestnut belongs to the genus Castanea of the beech family (Fagaceae) and widely cultivate in Europe, the U.S., China and Japan. Chestnuts generally range in height from 30 to 60 feet and have furrowed bark with toothed walnut or lance shaped leaves. The leaves are glossy and green but turn bronze in the fall. The staminate (male) flowers are borne in small spikes called catkins and the pistillate (female) flowers are hardly noticeable. The fruits are very spiny round burs, usually containing 2 or 3 shiny dark brown nuts.

The American chestnut one ranged throughout the eastern half of the U.S. and was one of the commonest trees there. Its wood was widely used for making rail fences and its nut were roasted and eaten by early settlers. Today the species most widely cultivated are the Spanish chestnut, the Japanese chestnut and especially the Chinese chestnut.

The horse-chestnut belongs to the family hippocastanaceae and the water-chestnut is an aquatic plant of the evening primrose family (Onagraceae). The cape chestnut is a tall South African tree while the Moveton Bay chestnut is a member of the legume family (Leguminosae).

90. Prune:

It is a member of the plum family (Prunus domestica) that are suitable for drying. As compared with the non-prune types of plum, prunes have firmer flesh and higher sugar content and can be dried without fermentation at the pit. A large part of the world's crop of prunes comes from the U.S. Other producers are France, Italy, Rumania, Czechoslovakia, Yugoslavia and Australia. It is not grown in India.

In processing dried prunes, the very ripe fruit is dipped in a weak solution of boiling lye, rinsed, and spread on drying trays, left for a day in the dehydration chamber, immersed in hot water or steam and packed. Prunes are very rich in vitamin A and a good source of vitamin B1 and B2. They also contain appreciable amounts of iron and calcium.

91. Pimento:

It is a kind of mild pepper of the genus capsicum, having distinctive flavour but lacking in pungency, so named from the Spanish word for pepper. These include European paprika which provide the paprika of commerce, a powdered red condiment.

92. Paprika:

It is a spice made by grinding large red fruits of the Capsicum annuum. Sweet and semi-sweet parprikas are mildly pungent, usually preferred in temperate climates; pungent paprika is a hot spice, usually preferred in tropical and sub-tripical zones.

The colour of paprika varies from a bright rich red in first quality products to a dull brick-red in products of inferior quality.

After picking, paprika pods are cured and dried in the sun or in artificially heated chamber. In California, pods are not cured but are dried with artificially heated forced air under controlled conditions, a process that requires only hours in contrast to days for the older method. First quality sweet paprika is prepared from pods divested of seeds, placenta tissue, calyces and stems.

93. Kale:

It is a biennial leafy vegetable, also called cole or colewort, native to northern Europe and British Isles. It was known to the ancient Greeks and Romans. Of all the sub-species of Brassica oleracea having economic importance, kale and collards most closely resemble the wild from. The plants are open, do not have head like cabbages and do not produce edible flowers like cauliflower and broccoli.

These are dwarf, medium high and tall varieties, with smooth, laciniated and curled leaves of lighter and darker shades of green, purple and variegated colours. In the U.S. kale and collards do better during warm weather but they also withstand considerable freezing and usually survive the winters in the south. They are extensively cultivated for their leafy greens. Kale is very rich in vitamins A and C. It also contains appreciable amounts of vitamins B1 and G.

94. Gourd (Kumro):

It is the name applied to plants and hard-shelled fruits of various species of the cucurbitaceae called the gourd family. The best known are the bottle or colabash gourd (Lagenaria siceraira) and the yellow-flowered ornamental gourd (Cucurbita pepe).

There is definite evidence that the fruits of the bottle gourd were used as utensils in the new world many centuries before the arrival of Columbus. Inspite of this, botanists believe that the bottle-gourd is native to Africa where many natural varieties occur throughout the central regions of the continent. Probably the fruits were carried to the New World long ago by ocean currents.

The bottle gourd is a hairy, rapid growing trailing or climbing annual herb, extending 30 feet or more in length. It has stout 5-angled stems, long-stalked, 5-lobed leaves and large yellow flowers. The fruits which may exceed 5 feet in length vary in shape. In India, their woody shells serve as utensils and as sounding boxes for the sitar and ektara used by the bauls of Bengal. The pulp of the fruit is eaten as a cooked vegetable. For raw juice purposes, this vegetable is not used.

95. Radish (Mula):

It is an annual or biennial plant grown for its large, succulent root. The edible part of the root, together with some of the seedling stem, forms a structure, varying in shape from spherical through oblong to long cylindrical or tapered. The outside colour of the root varies from white through pink to red, purple and black; the size of the edible fruit varies from a few grams to 2 kg. The seeds are borne in a pod called a silicle.

The small quick growing spring varieties have a mildly crisp, moderately firm flesh and are quickly perishable. The large slow growing summer and winter types have pungent, firm flesh. Winter varieties can be stored throughout the winter. The common radish is probably of oriental origin. The roots are usually eaten raw or cooked and the young tops are shredded and added to salads and curry.

Radish contains vitamin C in plenty and appreciable amounts of vitamin B1 and G, iron, potassium, sodium and magnesium which heal and soothe the mucous membranes. The juice of fresh radishes including the top is too potent to be taken alone. It should be mixed with carrot juice in order to have the effect of soothing and healing the membranes and cleansing the body of the mucus.

96. Lettuce:

It is a widely grown annual plant cultivated for the edible leaves. Lettuce leaves are low in calories but rich in vitamin A. It is believed that lettuce originally was native to Europe and Asia and was cultivated by 550 B.C. Today it is grown throughout the world.

Cultivated lettuce belongs to the composite family. After the leaves form, branching leafy flowering stems develop. These stems range in height 3 to 4 feet and bear cluster of small yellow flower heads.

There are four major botanical varieties of lettuce — Head or cabbage lettuce has a dense leafy head similar to that of cabbage. Head lettuce may be of four types, viz, butter-head, crisp-head, imperial and iceberg types. The second and third types have long shoe-horn shaped leaves. The fourth type lettuce or asparagus lettuce has thick edible stems but is rarely grown in the U.S.

Lettuce can be grown in a wide variety of soils including marshy and sandy, silty loams. Ample sunlight, uniformly cool nights and plenty of moisture are essential for well-developed lettuce heads. High temperature lead to inferior quality.

Lettuce contains vitamins A, B and C in plenty. It also contains calcium, iodine, magnesium and silicon. Lettuce juice has great quantities of iron and magnesium. Iron is the most active element in the body and it must be renewed and replenished more frequently than any other minerals. Iron is stored in the liver and spleen where it is ready to meet any sudden demand of the body such as the rapid formation of red blood corpuscles in heavy loss of blood.

The high content of magnesium in lettuce has exceptional vitalising powers specially in the muscular tissues, the brain and the nerves. Organic salts of magnesium are cell builders and they are very useful to the nerves. They help in maintaining the normal fluidity of the blood. When combined with carrot juice, the properties of lettuce are intensified by the addition of vitamin A and sodium.

Drinking daily an abundance of carrot, lettuce and spinach juice combined will supply food to the tired nerves and hair roots which is the only means by which the growth of hair can be stimulated. This juice combination is very helpful for maintaining the normal colour of the hair.

97. Leeks:

It is an onion like plant raised for its pungent leaves and long leaf stems. The leek (Allium possum) belongs to the lily family (Liliaceae) and is closely related to onion and garlic. Its stems are usually branched and both the stems and leaves are used as flavouring in soups and stews. The stems are also eaten raw as in salads or boiled and eaten like asparagus.

The leek is a hardy biennial believed to have originated in the Mediterrenean region. It is now grown in many parts of the world. Propagation is by seed which is often sown in early spring in a greenhouse or hot bed. The seedlings are then transplanted to a field in late spring. Sometimes the seed is sown directly in the field.

A deep loamy soil well supplied with moisture is essential for a good crop. The plants are spaced 3 to 6 inches apart in rows that are 15 inches apart. During the growing season, soil should be built up gradually around the stems of the plants to ensure branching. Too much soil around the young plants may cause the leaves to decay. The wild leek grows up to 10 inches tall and has onion-scented leaves and bulb and an umbel of white flowers. Leeks are very rich in vitamins A, B and C. It also contains iron in plenty.

98. Broccoli:

Botanically it is known as Brassica oleracea botrytis Linn. It is a fleshy-stemmed green food plant with flowering head. Broccoli probably originated from the wild cabbage common in coastal Europe. Ancestral forms of modern varieties seem to have been domesticated in Italy about the time of Christ.

The broccoli generally grown in Europe is different from that grown in North America. In the U.S. green sprouting varieties are mostly planted as summer annuals. In Europe, a hardier 'cauliflower' head type is grown, harvested in winter and spring, The broccoli grown in America became popular only within recent decades after it was shown that green vegetables have more vitamins that blanched vegetables.

Broccoli grows best in cool weather, in fertile soil, well-drained, amply watered soil. It can endure light frost. Seedlings are grown in glass enclosure and transplanted outdoor for summer harvest or they are planted directly outdoors for autumn harvest. Broccoli is cut before the flower buds open. When the terminal head is removed, small lateral shoots develop. In order to grow perfect heads, it is usually necessary to control cabbage worms, a common pest, by the application of an insecticide that is non-toxic to humans. Broccoli is very rich in vitamins A, B and C. It also contains potassium.

99. Asparagus:

Botanically it is known as Asparagus officinalis. It is an erect or climbing plant widely distributed from Siberia to South Africa. Some species such as the asparagus fern are often grown for their decorative value and one species is used in the flower trade, where it is called as 'sinilex'. The best known and the most widely cultivated species, however, is the common or garden asparagus where tender shoots or spears are widely eaten as vegetable.

The green shoots are usually sold fresh, while the white ones are used mostly for canning and freezing. A typical asparagus plant rises in height from either a tuberous root system or an underground stem called rhizome. Unlike most other plants, the asparagus does not produce true leaves. Instead it bears cladodes that produce many small scale-like structures called cadophylls which perform the function of true leaves. The flower of the asparagus is greenish yellow in colour and about 1/4 to 1/2 inch in length. They are borne singly or in short spikes or flat-topped clusters and in the fall each flower ripens into a small red berry.

The green shoots are low in calories but contain relatively large amounts of calcium and phosphorus. They also contain vitamins A and C and niacin. It is very valuable in scurvy, rickets, anaemia, pellagra and low vitality.

100. Turnip (Salgam):

Technically it is called Brassica rapa. Turnip is the popular name of the two closely related biennial herbs of the family Cruciferae. The common turnip has a flattened, white flashed tuberous root crowned by a compact tuft of thick green hairy leaves from the centre of which a flower stem rises about 18 inches and bears numerous yellow flowers. The Swedish turnip has a more globular yellow flashed root with a leafy neck and glaucous bluish, hairless cabbage-like leaves. Its flowers are also yellow.

The common turnip is a quick-growing plant sown as soon as the soil can be worked in spring or in midsummer. The first sowing produces roots for late spring and early summer use; the second for autumn consumption.

Turnips are very rich in vitamins A, B, C and G. They also contain calcium, sodium and sulphur. They are very useful in cases or rapid pulse, physical weakness, tender joints, stammering, catarrh, poor appetite and digestive disturbances.

Turnip leaves contain more calcium than any other vegetable. It is an excellent food for growing children and in softening of bones. The combination of turnip leaf juice and carrot and dandelion juice is one of the most effective means of hardening the teeth as well as the entire bone structure of the body. The high magnesium content of the dandelion together with the calcium in the turnip leaves and the element of the carrot combine to give this firmness and strength.

101. Okra or gumbo:

Technically it is known as Hibiscus esculentus. It is an annual plant of the mellow family, native to Africa, which grows to height of six feet and has yellow flower and large ovate leaves. Its mucilaginous pods are eaten in soups and stews as a vegetable. Okra is now extensively grown in the southern U.S. It is not found in India. Okra pods are very rich in vitamins A, B, C and G and minerals.

102. Spearmint:

Botanically it is called Mentha spicate. It is the common garden mint native to Europe and naturalised in North America. It is also known as greenmint and is very often found in damp places. It is cultivated for its very aromatic foliage, which are used to add zest to drinks such as the mint julap. The leaves yield an oil that is used as a flavouring and scent in chewing gums and other products and as herb seasoning for roast lamb.

Spearmint is about 2 feet tall. It has a smooth square stem and spreads by leafy stolons or runners. It has opposite, lance-shaped, sharply serrated, smoothish leaves and small two-lipped purplish flowers in slender spikes.

103. Sorrel:

It is a plant having in its leaves an acid sap that gives a sour flavour. The acidity may result from the presence of one or more organic acids, the commonest being citric, malic and oxalic. Common sorrel or sheep sorrel is a common pasture and roadside weed introduced from Europe and widely distributed in the U.S. Field sorrel is used for salads, soups and greens.

Indian or Jamaican sorrel called roselle is an East Indian mallow cultivated for its sour calyces which are used in drinks, jellies and tarts. Sweet sorrel is a common tropical and sub-tropical shrub with acid bitter foliage. Climbing sorrel climbs by rootlets.

104. Squash:

It is a vegetable plant similar to Indian gourd cultivated for food for man and livestock. Squashes range in size from a few inches to a foot in length. Some squashes have a white skin while others have skins of various colours, commonly yellow, tan or green. Squash plants have yellow male and female flowers that are borne singly in the axils of the leaves. Pollination is usually done by insects, chiefly bees.

Squashes are believed to have originated in South America, probably in Peru or Chile. Squashes are now grown in most parts of the world. The name 'squash' is applied to certain varieties of the species Cucurbita maxima.

Hibbard, delicious and butter-cup squashes are widely grown in home and nursery gardens of the U.S. The mammoth types of winter squashes are grown for stock-feed.

Straight neck and crooked-neck squashes are grown in summer. They are eaten when young and immature. Other kinds of summer squashes include Italian vegetable marrow, the cocozell, the zucchini and the English vegetable marrow. Squash is a rich source of vitamins A, B, C and G and minerals.

105. Zucchini:

It is a variety of summer squash of the Italian marrow type belonging to the Cucurbitaceae family. The bush type plant has short stems and deeply lobed leaves. The fruits are relatively short and cylindrical, of a creamy grey-green colour with darker green markings. The flesh is light greenish white when the fruits are small. The fruits are eaten when young and immature, boiled or steamed unpeeled.

Zucchini is very rich in vitamin A with considerable amounts of riboflavin, iron and calcium. It is very useful in low vitality, general debility, anaemia and run-down conditions.

The standard variety used by growers is the black zucchini with fruits coloured a deep dark green or nearly black. Troublesome pests are the squash bug, squash vine borer and cucumber beetle. Some of the diseases are bacterial wilt and mosaic.

106. Scallion:

It is a type of onion that has a thick base portion. It is also known as a green onion. The term scallion is also a applied to leeks and shallots. It is very rich in vitamins A, B1 and C. It also contains minerals and organic acids. Scallion is very useful in insomnia, arthritis, gout, sun-stroke, heat-stroke, allergy, heart-burn and dyspepsia.

107. Dill:

Botanically it is called Anethum graveolens. Dill is the common name of a Eurasian annual or biennial herb belonging to the parsley family. It is widely used for seasoning food. The dill plant grows up to 3-4 feet high and has a long-spindle shaped root, a branched stem, fine divided leaves and compound clusters of yellow flowers. Although the entire plant is aromatic, the largest amount of volatile oil of dill (Oleven amethi) is present in the seeds. Dill oil, a minor essential oil, is produced by steam distillation from the herb and from the mature fruit. The main constituent is carvone.

Dill has been cultivated in the Mediterranean area since ancient times. It is also now grown in many other parts of Europe, in the United States and in India. The young leaves and the seeds are used for seasoning foods. Dill vinegar, made by steeping the seeds in vinegar for several days, is used for flavouring and pickling. Dill seeds are also used medicinally for their carminative or gas-expelling properties.

Dill plant is a rich source of vitamins and minerals. It is very useful in liver and stomach disorders.

108. Water lily (Sapla):

It is a plant of the aquatic family Nymphaceae. These are found in fresh, still waters throughout the warm and temperate regions and often cultivated. Some can be raised easily from the seed. They may be grown in tanks or even in half-barrels as well as in ponds. The water-lilies are handsome plants having more or less orbicular leaves either floating or immersed and solitary flowers. The fruit is indehiscent, fleshy and like a large berry filled with seeds. The seeds have small embryo and abundant starchy perisperm and enclosed in palpy arils. When the seeds are ripe, pods break open irregularly. The seeds are borne to the surface of the water by the buoyant arils where they repel each other and float far and wide by currents of water and wind. After one or two hours, the aril contracts and breaks loose and lets the seeds to drop to the bottom of the pond. The stem is eaten as a vegetable which contains some vitamins and minerals. This plant is not so useful for healing purposes.

109. Taro, arum (Kachu):

Botanically it is known as Colocasia esculente. It is a member of the arum family (Araceae). It is a large-leaved tropical plant that has been grown as a staple food crop in the orient for more than 2000 years. Although all parts of the plant are edible, it is grown mainly for its fleshy underground corms and tubers which are rich in starch and protein and are usually eaten like potato or used to make flour. Taros are richer than potatoes in carbohydrates and most vitamins and minerals.

The corms and tubers as well as other parts contain needle-like crystals of calcium oxalate that give the plant a bitter taste or itching sensation in the throat. It can be removed by boiling. The leaves and leafstalks are very rich in vitamin C and are eaten as green vegetables. It is an erect plant that rises from 3 to 7 ft. Its whorled leaves are attached near the centre of the blades to the long thick leafstalks. It is originated in Malaysia, India and Indonesia and then introduced in other parts of the world.

110. Kohlrabi:

It is a vegetable plant of the cabbage variety from which it differs in the swelled, turnip-like stem with a tuft of loose leaves on the top. This bulbous stem which may be six inches in diameter is used for human and as stock-food in America and Europe. Kohlrabi is a very rich source of vitamin C and minerals.

111. Marjoram :

It is the common name for a sub-shrub and perennial herb of the genus Origanum comprising about 25 species in the mint family (Labiatae) and is usually found in the Meditarranean region. Especially important is the common or pot marjoram — an erect, branching, aromatic perennial found wild on dry pastures and hedges from Britain to central Europe to Himalayas. It stands about 30 inches high; has hairy ovate, slightly toothed leaves 1-1/2 inches long and dense clusters of rose purple flowers. It is widely cultivated and its leaves are used fresh or dried as seasoning for meats, salads, sauces and other foods. Marjoram contains some of the vitamins and minerals.

112. Chicory:

It is a perennial plant whose leaves are widely eaten as salad greens or as a cooked vegetable. The chicory, also called witloof, is cultivated in Europe and Asia. It ranges in height from 3 to 6 ft. and bears bright blue flower heads. The fleshy roots of the chicory are dried, ground and roasted to be used as a flavouring or adulterant to coffee.

When grown for its leaves, chicory seed is planted in spring in rows 15 to 18 inches apart. Just before cold weather, the roots are harvested and the tops are cut off about 2 inches above the crown. The roots may be placed in cold storage until they are used.

The chicory is botanically called as Cichorium intybus and belongs to the composite family. It is closely related to endive and is sometimes called French endive. It is a very rich source of vitamins A, B, C and G. It also contains minerals. Its drink as coffee is stimulant and envigorating. It increases stamina and vigour, vitality and strength.

113. Rutabaga:

It is an edible plant closely related to the turnip and usually cultivated for its smooth, thick, yellow or white tuber or underground stem which is fed to livestock and also eaten by man.

Botanically it is known as Brassica napoorasico. It is a member of the mustard family Cruciferae. It usually grows to height of 3 feet and has long thick, shiny bluish green leaves and yellowish flowers. It grow best in northern areas of Europe with a cool climate. The flesh of the tuber is solid, stored well and has characteristic sweet flavour. It is a rich source of vitamin C. It also contains some minerals.

114. Fennel (Madhumika):

Botanically it is known as Foeniculum vulgare. It is a tall herb of the carrot family (Umbelliferae) found in southern Europe but also grows in other parts of the world including India. All portions of the shoot are aromatic and can be utilised in various ways. The young leaves and the seeds are used as culinary herb to give flavour to sauces, soups, chowders and other dishes and for flavouring candy and liquors. An oil extracted from the fruit is used in perfumes, soaps and medicines. The thick leafstalks of the finocchio or Florence variety are blanched and used like celery.

Fennel usually grows to a height of few feet and has finely divided leaves and yellow flowers. It is a perennial plant but commonly treated as an annual when grown as a garden herb.

It is a rich source of vitamin C and is very useful in bronchitis, scurvy, rapid pulse, low vitality, tender joints, restlessness, impaired digestion and physical weakness.

It is also very useful in amenorrhoea as it promotes menstrual regularity. The oil from the seed is very useful in removing hookworms. It is rich in all the most valuable elements and vitamins and when mixed with carrot juice is a great aid in night blindness and other eye troubles.

115. Brussels sprouts:

Technically it is known as Brassica oleracea gemmifer De candolle. It is a green food plant that bears small heads or sprouts. It probably mutated from a primitive cabbage similar to collard (a large kale) sometimes in the 14th century, near Brussels, Belgium. The Brussels sprouts are tall cabbages in which many individual, miniature cabbage heads, rather than single terminal head, develop at the stem joints where leaves have been shed.

Brussels sprouts are grown best in rich, loamy, amply watered soil. They are generally started under glass and transplanted outdoors. Light frost is not injurious to Brussels sprouts and is said to improve their flavour. In cold climates, they can be planted directly outdoor early in spring. Only 130 days is required from planting to harvest. Brussels sprouts are picked individually as they mature, younger ones maturing progressively higher on the stem.

It is a very rich source of vitamin A, B, and C and minerals. It is specially useful in gastric and peptic ulcer.

It is said that string beans and Brussels sprouts furnish a natural insulin for the pancreatic functions of the digestive organs. It is very useful for diabetic patients.

116. Caper:

Botanically it is called Caparis spinosa, a member of the caper family, grows to 4 ft. tall and produces quickly fading 4-petalled white flowers. The flowers which bear masses or showy stamens that extend well beyond the petals mature into berries with numerous seeds.

117. Black pepper (Kalajira):

Black pepper is the most used spice in the world today for its medicinal properties. This plant is widely grown in Indonesia, India, Thailand and the East

Indies. It was also introduced in the western hemisphere.

It is a woody climber and may attain a height of 33 feet by means of its arial roots. Its broad and shiny green leaves are alternately arranged. The flowers are in dense slender spikes of about 50 blossoms each. The berrylike fruits or pepper corns are nearly globular, about 0.2 inch in diameter. They become yellowish red at maturity and bear a single seed. Their odour is penetrating and aromatic; the taste is hot, biting and very pungent. The berries are picked when they begin to turn red, immersed in boiling water for about 10 minutes which makes them turn dark brown or black in an hour. They are then spread on the floor to dry.

In ancient times, the black pepper was used as a cure for headache, blood dysentery, scarlet fever, small-pox, leprosy, typhus, cholera and plague.

118. Ginger (Ada, adrak):

Botanically it is called as Zingiber officinale, of the family Zingiberaceae. It is a perennial plant widely cultivated in Asia for its aromatic, pungent rhizome (underground stem) used as a spice, flavouring food and medicine. Its use in India and China has been known from ancient times and by the first century A.D. traders had taken ginger to the Mediterranean region. By the 11th century, it was well-known in England. The Spaniards brought it to the West Indies and Mexico soon after their conquest and by 1547 ginger was being exported from Santiago to Spain.

The spice has a pleasant, slightly biting taste and is usually dried and ground to flavour breads, sauces, curry dishes, confections, pickles and ginger ale. The fresh rhizome is used in cooking. The peeled rhizomes may be preserved by boiling in syrup. Medically it is used in fever, cough and cold, influenza, flatulence and colic.

Ginger contains 2% of essential oil, the principle of the spice is zingerone. The oil is distilled from the rhizomes for use in the food and perfume industry. In ancient times, raw ginger was used as a breath sweetener, an aid to digestion, a cure for toothache and bleeding gums and as a strengthening agent for loose teeth and weak eyes.

119. Cloves (Labanga):

Botanically it is called Syzygium aromaticum. It is the dried flower bud of the clove tree. Cloves have long been valued for their spicy flavour. They were used in China as early as 3rd century B.C. and were introduced in Europe during the middle ages. Cloves either whole or ground are used as pickling spice as well as for flavouring vermouth, and in the orient as an ingredient in some chewing and smoking tobaccos. Clove oil is used as a cleaning agent in the preparation of slides for microscopic examination and as an antiseptic in dentistry.

The trees were originally found in the Moluccas Islands and were later introduced in other parts of the tropical regions. The world's leading producer is the Island of Zanzibar. Other exporters of clove are Indonesia, Madagascar, Mauritius and Reunion.

It is an evergreen tree with smooth grey bark. Cultivated trees are usually 25 to 49 ft. high but wild trees may attain a height of 60 ft. or more. The trees are grown from seed and begin to produce flowers when about 8 or 9 years old. They continue to produce flowers for 50 years or more. Clove trees thrive in fertile loamy soil at altitudes up to 2000 ft. in tropical regions having an annual rainfall between 50 to 70 inches.

In ancient times, cloves were used as a breath sweetener, a comforter for heart, liver, stomach, and bowels; a remedy for nausea, colic, flatulence, toothache, and diarrhoea; a preventive for paralysis of the tongue; inflammation of the gums and loosening of the teeth. Rose water flavoured with cloves is a favourite eye-wash.

120. Cardamon (Elachi):

Its botanical name is Elettaric cardamomum. It is a herb with seeds that are used as a spice and in medicine. It grows 5 to 9 feet high and has course leaves 2-1/2 feet long. The white flowers are borne in loose, irregular spikes about 2 feet long. The rootstock is thick and creeping.

Cardamon grows easily in moist mild climates, specially in shaded situations. It is commonly cultivated in Jamaica and is sometimes raised in greenhouses. It is easily propagated by seeds and division of roots. Cardamon becomes exhausted after bearing 3 or 4 crops. It is also grown in India. In ancient times, the dried seeds were used in asthma, bronchitis, piles, diseases of the bladder, headache, earache and toothache. The seeds were also used in flatulence and dyspepsia.

121. Cinnamon (Daruchini):

Its botanical name is Cinnamonum zeylanicum. It is the dried, highly aromatic, reddish or yellowish brown bark of the cinnamon tree. It has long been valued as a spice. The ancient Greeks and Romans obtained it from Arabian traders. The Portuguese in their attempt to find the source of cinnamon and other spices, discovered the route around Cape Horn to India and Ceylon in 1505.

Wild cinnamon trees may attain a height of 30 feet or more but under cultivation, they are trained or pruned. When the shoots are about 6 to 8 feet high, they are cut off near the ground. Harvesting is done during the rainy season, because the bark is more easily stripped from shoots that are undergoing rapid growth. To facilitate stripping, the bark is slit along the length of the stem on each side. The bark is then pried loose at one end of the shoot and peeled off. The stripes are heaped together and covered with sacks to promote fermentation which loosens the corky outer layer of the bark so that it may be readily scraped off. It is the inner bark that contains the aromatic properties. Cinnamon oil is obtained by the distillation of shoots and low grade bark. Cinnamon oil is used mostly as a flavouring in medicine. It may also be used as an astrigent or to relieve excess gas in the stomach and intestines. In ancient times, the oil was used in amenorrhoea and gonorrhoea. It was also used as a liniment in rheumatic pains, headache and toothache.

122. Cassava, tapioca, manioc, mandioc, yuca:

Botanically it is called Manihot esculenta, a member of the flowering plant family Euphorbiacea from the American tropics. It is usually grown throughout the tropical world for its tuberous roots from which cassava flour, breads, tapioca, a laundry starch and even an alcoholic beverage are derived. Cassava first originated at Yucatan and later was introduced in other parts of the world. A cyanide-producing sugar derivative is also found in the roots in most varieties. Primitive peoples developed a complex refining system to remove the poison by grating, pressing and heating the tubers.

It is a perennial with conspicuous, almost fan-shaped leaves (like castor bean) but more deeply parted into 5 to 9 lobes. The fleshy roots are reminiscent of dahlia tubers. Ceara rubber is produced from a specie called Manihot glaziovil in Brazil. Food items such as the glatinous fufu of West Africa and the baumi mush of Jamaica come from cassava. Additional cassava products include an alcoholic beverage made by Indians in South America. The powdery cassabe cakes of Yucatan and tapioca are the only cassava products available in Northern markets.

123. Hickory nuts:

Botanically it is called Carya ovata in the walnut family (Juglandaceae). These trees are extensively cultivated in the United States, Canada, Mexico and China for its wood and nut. Hickory wood is coarse, straight, grained and shock resistant and among the toughest, hardest and strongest of woods. It is used in sports equipment and veneers and as timber, charcoal and for smoking meats. Hickory nuts are important game food; even the bitter nuts are eaten. The players love it very much as it increases strength, vitality and vigour which are essential requirements of a player.

124. Girasole or Jerusalem artichoke:

The vegetable, resembling a potato, is served cooked. The carbohydrate insulin stored in this tuber yields fructose useful in the treatment of diabetes. It is a tuber-bearing sunflower native to North America. The above green part of the plant is a coarse, usually multi-branched, frost-tender annual, 7 to 10 feet tall, numerous showy flowerheads appearing in late summer or early autumn, have yellow ray-flowers. The underground tubers vary from oblong to much elongated regular to rough and branched. Jerusalem artichokes are very popular as cooked vegetable in Europe and have long been cultivated in France as a stock feed. In the United States, it is rarely cultivated but small quantities are used in making pickles, relishes and dietary preparations.

125. Escarole:

It is a leafy annual or biennial plant closely related to chicory and widely used in salads. It is better known as endive. This plant is cultivated only in Europe and America.

FRUIT AND VEGETABLE JUICE FORMULAS FOR SPECIFIC AILMENTS

Dr. Stanley Davidson has said, 'Germs do not cause disease but they appear in the same way as flies do when garbage is lying about. Where there is garbage, there are flies or germs. So if the human body is kept free from any garbage or filth or waste products, then it can remain free of disease'. So it is the elimination of accumulated waste products, or garbage inside the body which is of utmost importance. Diseases will automatically disappear if the body is always kept clean or free from any garbage or waste products.

Raw fruit juice therapy is the best or right way to remove such bodily filth or waste materials most effectively in a natural way without any after-effects.

Hippocrates, the father of medicine, has said, 'If anyone can take a glass of musumbi or narangi juice once a week in the morning, he can keep himself free from any disease.' If he can keep himself free from any disease, he can work more, earn more, enjoy more and live for more days in this world.

Dr. John B. Lust has said, 'Natural healing is the most desirable factor in the regeneration of the race. It is a return to nature in methods of living and treatment. It makes use of the elementary forces of nature, of chemical selection of foods that will constitute a correct medical dietary.'

Dr. Louis Kulne in his book 'The New science healing' has observed that toxic accumulation in the human body is the root cause of all diseases. Such accumulations are reabsorbed in the blood stream and they cause all ailments in the body. So the proper method to remain free from any disease is to detoxify the whole body by means of consuming fresh fruit or vegetable juice in the morning.

What is the most perfect food? The answer will be: What the nature has provided us. Food as it grows.

1. **Acne; pimples :** It is a skin disease caused by blood impurities which the body is trying to eliminate through the skin.

   Lime (musumbi), cucumber, marmelos and papaya juice (16 ounces a day).

2. **Adenoids:** It is caused by inflammation of pharyngeal tonsil or adenoid tissue. Children often have enlarged tonsils.

   Carrot, beet, lime and orange juice.

3. **Allergy:** It is caused by sensitiveness to certain foods like eggs, prawn, meat, beet, carrot etc. which may produce skin eruption, hay fever, eczema, nettle-rash etc. Another important cause is said to be presence of excessive heat in the body.

   Lemon, marmelos, papaya and cucumber juice (16 ounces a day).

4. **Anaemia:** It is usually caused by iron deficiency. The relatively small amount of iron needed for manufacture of haemoglobin is missing. This is the essential element in the red blood cell and is responsible for the transport of oxygen from the lungs to other body cells.

   Apple, lime (musumbi), carrot, beet, and spinach juice (16 ounces a day).

5. **Amenorrhoea:** Absence of monthly flow; severe pain; less blood.

   Fig (dumur) or fennel juice regularises menstrual flow.

6. **Angina pectoris:** Vulvular or muscular heart trouble resulting from impurities in the blood stream.

   Lime (musumbi), garlic, onion and cucumber juice.

7. **Appedicitis:** It is inflammation of the appendix. Pain in the right side is one of the common symptoms of this disease. Other symptoms are vomiting, sweating and dizziness.

   Garlic, lime (musumbi), onion and tomato juice.

8. **Appetite loss:** Juice of orange, lemon, marmelos, tomato and garlic.

9. **Arthritis:** It refers to inflammation of joints with severe pain. It is caused due to inorganic

calcium in the cartilege of the joints as a result of eating carbohydrates and meat in excess.

Garlic, lime (narangi), onion, bitter gourd (karela), margosa and lemon juice.

10. **Ascites:** Painless swelling of the abdomen as a result of accumulation of fluid therein.

    Juice of lemon, musumbi, tomato, papaya and marmelos.

11. **Asthma:** Acute difficulty in breathing at night due to mucus accumulation in bronchial tubes.

    Juice of orange, carrot, beet, garlic, onion, and spinach. A few slices of onion should be taken at supper time along with a few cloves of garlic in order to get sound sleep at night.

12. **Backache:** Pain in the back is one of the commonest complaints doctors have to deal with. It is primarily caused by deep-seated mental stress or hidden emotional conflict projected on the back.

    Juice of garlic, orange, bitter-gourd, margosa leaves, carrot and beet.

13. **Beriberi:** It is a vitamin B1 (thiamine) deficiency disease and characterised by inflammatory changes in the nerves.

    Juice of garlic, musumbi, bitter-gourd, lemon, margosa leaves.

14. **Biliousness:** It is a condition of general discomfort popularly attributed to an excess of bile in the system.

    Juice of musumbi, tomato, papaya, marmelos, lemon.

    A few slices of marmalades of marmelos fruit will be very useful (beler morobba).

15. **Bites of insects and stings of scorpions:** If you apply garlic juice to the affected part, you will get instant relief.

16. **Bladder trouble:** It denotes difficulties or abnormalities in passing urine.

    Lime (musumbi), cashew nut, garlic, lemon, papaya and marmelos juice.

17. **Bleeding:** If you apply camphor powder to the affected part the bleeding will stop instantly.

18. **Blood pressure high:** High blood pressure is excessive tension of blood in the arteries caused by improper diet, lack of exercise and to a lesser extent by neurasthenia, worry, and anxiety.

    Garlic, tomato, marmelos, papaya, lime (musumbi) and orange (narangi) juice. A few cloves of garlic should be chewed daily in the morning.

19. **Blood pressure low:** It may be caused due to excessive use of devitalising foods in the diet, resulting in deficiency of vital elements in the

blood stream. Actually it is caused by malnutrition.

Carrot, beet, spinach, grape, apple and musumbi juice.

20. **Burns:** Apply crushed potato juice in the burns and then leave it bandaged for a day, you will find prompt relief.

21. **Boil and abscess:** They are caused by impurities in the blood resulting in bacterial infection through the sweat glands or the follicles of the hair.

    Garlic, water-melon, cucumber, marmelos and onion juice. Crushed garlic juice may be applied locally on the boils.

22. **Bronchitis:** It is inflammation of the bronchial tubes following common cold or other infection of the respiratory tract.

    Carrot, beet, orange, grape and spinach juice. A few cloves of garlic should be chewed daily in the morning for some time.

23. **Cancer:** A malignant tumour may ultimately develop into cancer. Cancer is characterised by growth of unwanted cells which sucks the vital nutrients of the body causing death of the patient. It may appear in any part of the body. Cancer in different parts has different names like carcinoma, sarcoma, melanoma, leukaemia etc.

Carcinoma is cancer of the skin, glands, or membranes; sarcoma is cancer of the bone, muscle or connective tissue; melenoma is cancer of the lymphatic nodes and leukaemia is cancer of the blood. Mostly cancer occurs after middle age and in late life. Nowadays children and young people under 21 are also stricken with cancer.

Cancer is usually caused by constant consumption of devitalised or adulterated foods. Some doctors have opined that this is a vitamin deficiency disease. Others have expressed the view that it is a disease of malnutrition. Syphilitic lesions of the tongue may lead to cancer of the tongue. Prolonged exposure to sun's rays causes skin cancer. Alcohol if taken in excess causes cancer of the larynx and liver. Cigarette smoking appears to be factor in lung cancer. Chewing betel leaves with tobacco mixture (gundi) may develop cancer of the mouth and liver. Chewing dried tobacco leaves with lime (chun) may cause cancer of the tongue and liver. Frequent childbirth may develop cancer of the uterus.

Medical science has completely failed to provide any relief. Some doctors like Dr. Eva Hill, Dr. Harry Hoxsey, Dr. Max Garson etc. resorted to raw juice therapy and were crowned with success.

The whole body is required to be detoxified by consuming raw fruit juices like lime (musumbi), orange (narangi), garlic, onion, lemon, pineapple. Crushed garlic may be applied externally on the affected part to be fixed with a sticking plaster and to be renewed every four hours till complete recovery. Dr. Harry Hoxsey became successful in his attempt to follow this procedure. He recorded his observation in his famous book, 'You don't have to die'. He was convicted by the U.S. Govt. and later his conviction was quashed. He proved by actual experiment that cancer can be cured by raw juice therapy. His theory is really very wonderful. This is a new hope to mankind in general.

Dr. E. C. Cowdrey in his book 'Trends in Cancer Research' has said, 'One of the 20 chief achievements since 1938 in cancer research is proof that dietary factors influence cancer promotion'. He also confirmed the view that cancer is caused by consuming devitalised foods and vegetables cooked by irrational preparation. Raw fruit juices can keep you in good health and will certainly increase your longevity.

Dr. Cyrin Scott in his book 'Victory over cancer' has said, 'According to reliable statistics, more than 600 persons die every day from cancer in the U.S. One out of every five Americans will eventually have cancer. This killer claims the life of one American in every two or three minutes. Since the year 1900, cancer has risen from the 8th position as the cause of death to second place, heart-attack being the first and alcoholism the third.' In India cancer ranks second as the cause of death. Heart-attack claims to be the first.

Dr. Eva Hill, a cancer specialist of the Auckland General Hospital, New York has expressed the view that cancer is only one of the degenerative diseases increasingly afflicting those who eat and drink unnatural foods dosed with pesticides and reared on or grown on depleted soil.

Dr. J. P. Davidson, a cancer specialist of the U.S., has opined that cancer is caused due to malnutrition. It is practically a vitamin deficiency disease. He advised all cancer patients to live mainly on raw fresh fruit and vegetable juices and no cereals. He made experiments and found that cancer patients if kept on raw fresh fruit and vegetable juices showed remarkable improvement. He had not given any cereals to them during treatment.

Dr. Max Garson, a cancer specialist of the U.S., has expressed the view that in cancer, as in all degenerative diseases, not only the affected part but the whole body must be treated. Cancer does not need specific treatment. It is a degenerative disease and has to be treated with raw fruit juice therapy so that the whole body is detoxified most effectively. He selected potassium iodide mixed with fruit juices and found excellent results. Detoxification of the whole body is the only answer. He believed that there was no drug which could cure cancer fully. Only raw fresh fruit and vegetable juices can treat cancer patients most effectively.

Juice of garlic, musumbi, orange, pineapple, papaya, tomato, marmelos, spinach, carrot, beet in plenty. Crushed garlic may be applied externally on the affected part in case of skin cancer.

24. **Catarrh:** This refers to inflammatory discharge from a mucous membrane, i.e. running nose and other symptoms of common cold.

    Lime (musumbi), orange (narangi), garlic, apple, and grape juice. Liquorice with honey may be found useful. Ginger and basil leaves with honey may be taken.

25. **Cold and cough:** These are caused due to deficiency of vitamins and minerals; Sometimes due to change of weather.

    Lime (musumbi), orange (narangi), garlic, apple and grape juice. Liquorice with honey may be found useful. Ginger with basil leaves and honey may be taken.

26. **Constipation:** Sluggishness of bowel movement.

    Musumbi, pineapple and lemon juice.

27. **Corns:** They are thickenings of the outer layer of the skin due to persistent friction and pressure. They are irritating and painful because the horny, hardened skin presses on nerve endings. The corn is usually cone-shaped.

    If you apply lemon juice externally on the affected part, you will get instant relief.

28. **Defective vision:** Impaired vision.

    Carrot, beet, orange juice.

29. **Diabetes:** It is a disease when the body is unable to manage or metabolise the food properly. It is classified as a nutritional or metabolic or insulin deficiency disease.

    Lime (musumbi), lemon, tomato, orange (narangi), marmelos, papaya, garlic juice. A glass of musumbi juice daily in the morning will give instant relief.

30. **Diarrhoea:** Looseness of bowel movements arises from a variety of causes like over-eating, food-poisoning, abuse of cathertic drugs, emotional stress, fatigue and change of weather.

    One glass of musumbi juice should be taken in the morning. Marmalades of raw marmelos (beler morabba) should be taken for some time. Half-ripe tomatoes are also useful. A soup of green papaya or green plantain will be helpful.

31. **Dysentery:** It is bowel disorder characterised by pain in the abdomen, diarrhoea, cramps and sometimes bloody or mucous stools. It is a very common disease during rainy season.

    One glass of musumbi juice should be taken in the morning. Marmalades of raw marmelos (beler morabba) should be taken for some time. Half-ripe tomatoes are also useful. A soup of green papaya or plantain, and Indian pennywort will be very helpful.

32. **Eye troubles:** It is a vitamin A and iron deficiency disease. It is also caused by eye strain, poor light, glare.

    Carrot, orange, beet and spinach juice.

33. **Fatigue or stress:** General weakness.

    Carrot, beet, orange, grape and apple juice.

34. **Fever:** Abnormal increase in body temperature due to a variety of causes.

    Orange, grape, apple, carrot and beet juice. Liquorice with honey will be very helpful. Ginger and basil leaves may be taken.

35. **Gastric ulcer:** Ulceration of the stomach.

    Cabbage juice will be highly effective in gastric ulcer. Half-boiled green papaya and plantain (kanchkala) will be very helpful. Marmaledes of raw marmelos should be taken daily.

    Dr. Garnett Cheney made extensive research and found that cabbage juice would cure gastric ulcer. The healing agent vitamin U had been isolated and identified by him. He observed that anti-ulcer factor vitamin U is destroyed by fire or cooking. So he gave his patients to drink raw cabbage juice with remarkable success.

    Marmalades of raw marmelos should be taken daily. Green papaya and green plantain boiled or in a soup should be taken. A glass of musumbi juice should be taken in the morning.

36. **General debility:** Weakness.

    Musumbi, orange, carrot, beet, apple and grape juice.

37. **Goitre:** Enlargement of the thyroid gland due to lack of iodine.

    Garlic, lime, orange and lemon juice.

38. **Gout:** It is caused due to excess of uric acid in the joints. Symptoms are inflammation of the joints with severe pain.

    Garlic, lime, orange, carrot, beet and lemon juice. Fried garlic cloves should be taken daily.

    Gout is a disturbance in metabolism. The metabolic abnormality results from an unusual use of certain foods (purines) so that the end product of purine metabolism (uric acid) is present in the blood in increased amounts. Purines are found in most kinds of meat, especially in the red meat from hogs and cattle. This factor establishes a definite relationship between gout and meat eating — The New York Times dt. 18.7.1971.

39. **Headache:** A cool and refreshing drink made of green coconut, cucumber, water-melon and peppermint will be very helpful if taken after a cold bath. Avoid tea or coffee.

40. **Heartburn:** It refers to a burning sensation in the food tube located near the heart.

Lime or lemon juice will be very useful. Tomatoes, marmelos, papaya, cucumber may be taken.

41. **Heart-attack:** The chief causes of heart-attack are obesity, strain, stress, anxiety, fast living, consumption of more fat and cholesterol containing foods life beaf, mutton, bacon, chicken, lobster, shrimp, oyster, duck, goose, cheese, butter, ghee, dalda, coconut oil etc. It is certainly a disease. We inherit certain diseases like asthma, heart diseases, iron deficiency, nervous disorders etc. from our parents. It is usually caused due to high blood pressure. Heart-attack ranks first as cause of death today. Cancer comes second and diabetes third.

Musumbi, lemon and narangi juice.

A vegetarian diet can prevent 90% of our thrombo-embolic diseases and 27% of other coronary occlusions. High levels of cholesterol in the blood have been linked to increased chances of developing heart disease. Consumption of meat daily may develop heart trouble very rapidly. — Journal of American Medical Association dt. 3.6.1961.

Drs. Hardinge and Stone made researches and found that plant proteins produce lower levels of cholesterol in the blood than animal protein. They advised heart patients not to consume meat but to take as much fruit juices as practicable.

Albert Einstein, the renowned scientist and Nobel Laureate has said, 'It is my view that the vegetarian manner of living by its purely physical effect on the human temperament would most beneficially improve the lot of mankind.'

Dr. David Cargill in his book 'How to avoid a coronary thrombosis' has said that consumption of meat like mutton, chicken, bacon, pork, hog etc. will increase the cholesterol content of the blood which may cause rapid coronary attacks. He also advised that heart patients should consume less fat and cholesterol containing foods. According to him, raw fruit juice will be most beneficial to all heart patients.

Dr. Lawrence E. Lamb in his book 'Your heart and how to live with it' has also confirmed the above view. He also advised that heart patients should consume raw fruit and vegetable juice as much as possible. They should always avoid meat of all kinds and try to live on vegetarian diet.

Dr. Robert Allen Miller in his book 'How to live with a heart attack' has remarked that saturated fats like cream, butter, ghee, margarine, coconut oil, vegetable oil (dalda) are very harmful to heart patients. But unsaturated fats like maize oil, sunflower oil, til oil, gingelly, mustard oil are not bad and they contain less fat and less cholesterol. He was also of the view that raw fruit juice played an important part in the life of heart patients.

42. **Impotency:** Male inability to perform the sexual act.

Walnut, cashew nut, pea-nut, chestnut, pistachio, hickory nut, mango, grape, orange and pea.

43. **Insomnia:** Inability to sleep properly at night. If you eat fried garlic (a few cloves) at supper time and one raw onion, you will surely get a sound sleep. It is not necessary to take sleeping pills.

44. **Liver troubles:** Abnormalities of the stomach functions.

    It is necessary to sip a glass of musumbi juice in the morning for some time. Marmalades of raw marmelos (beler morabba) will be very useful. A soup made of green papaya and green plantain will be very useful. Tomatoes (half-ripe) also will be very useful.

45. **Loss of memory:** Lime, orange, grape, garlic and lemon juice.

46. **Low vitality:** General debility.

    Orange, grape, apple, carrot and beet juice.

47. **Menorrhagia:** Excessive bleeding during menses.

    Plantain flower (mocha), and fig (dumur) juice will be highly effective in reducing menstrual bleeding. Orange, lime, apple and garlic juice will also be useful.

48. **Ophthalmia:** It is also known as conjunctivitis, i.e. inflammation of the eyes.

Cucumber, tomato, marmelos, papaya and onion juice.

49. **Peptic ulcer:** Ulceration of the stomach.

    Raw cabbage juice should be taken for some time. A soup made of green papaya and green plantain will be very useful. A glass of musumbi juice should be taken in the morning. Mamalades of raw marmelos (beler morabba) will give you instant relief.

50. **Prostate gland disorder:** Difficulty in urination.

    Garlic, lemon, lime (musumbi) and orange juice.

51. **Rheumatism:** Excess of uric acid in the joints.

    Garlic, musumbi, orange, tomato and lemon juice. Avoid meat diet as far as practicable.

52. **Rickets:** Deficiency in calcium, vitamins and minerals, especially lack of vitamin D.

    Vitamin D is practically absent in fruits and vegetables. Sunbath is essential. However the juice of musumbi, orange, grape and garlic will be very useful.

53. **Scurvy:** It is practically caused by deficiency of vitamin C. Usual symptoms are swollen and bleeding gums, black and blue spots on the skin, anaemia, rapid heart, loose teeth, sore arms and legs and extreme weakness.

Garlic, musumbi, orange and lemon juice (16 ounces daily).

54. **Sinus trouble:** It originates from common cold.

    Garlic, orange, lemon, apple and musumbi juice.

55. **Sciatica:** It is a form of neuritis involving pain along the course of sciatic nerves, the longest nerve in the body which runs down the back of the thigh to the legs.

    Garlic, musumbi, orange and lemon juice.

56. **Sore throat:** Inflammation of the walls of the throat.

    Garlic, musumbi, orange and lemon juice.

57. **Teeth:** Calcium and phosphorus are specially necessary to make the teeth strong. Vitamins and minerals are also necessary.

    If you take a few cloves of fried garlic every day, you will surely get instant relief. Musumbi, orange, lemon juice will be very useful.

58. **Tonsillitis:** It is an inflammation of the two almond shaped glands one each side of the throat. It is caused by deficiency of vitamins and minerals.

    Garlic, musumbi, orange and lemon juice.

59. **Travel sickness:** Uneasiness and vomiting during travel.

    Lemon and musumbi juice.

60. **Tumour:** It may be in bones, in liver and in uterus. They are unusual growths of cells due to a lack of sufficient organic elements and caused by the excessive use of devitalising foods. A malignant tumour may turn into cancer. Medical men found on research that an imbalance in the body chemistry and cell metabolism caused all sorts of degenerative diseases like cancer, arthritis and heart disease. They also found that detoxification of the whole body would cure such diseases. Detoxification of the whole body can be done by consuming raw fruit juice in adequate quantities. So the key-word is DETOXIFICATION.

Carrot, beet, musumbi, orange, garlic, onion and lemon juice.

Dr. S. Firenczi, a cancer specialist of Hungary, found beet juice most efficient in curing various sorts of tumours. One half to one kilogram daily of raw beet juice in small doses after meals and between meals were given to tumour patients. Sometimes he gave raw beet juice diluted in water. He found remarkable results in 15 out of 16 cases; the cancerous growths disappeared in a very short time. His findings will bring a new hope for the suffering mankind in general.

61. **Vomiting:** Ejection by way of mouth of stomach contents.

Lemon and musumbi juice will be very helpful.

62. **Weakness:** Musumbi, carrot, beet, orange, lemon, grape and apple juice.

63. **Worms:** Chirata and lime water taken in the morning destroys worms. Raw bitter-gourd (karela) or margosa leaf (neem) juice will also be very useful.

BRIEF NOTES ON VITAMINS

'Both vitamins and minerals are necessary to a well-balanced diet. As a matter of fact, vitamins control your body's utilization of minerals. In addition, each vitamin seems to have a specific role to play in normal body function. On the other hand, if the mineral supply is deficient, there is little benefit from the vitamins. Without vitamins, your body can still appropriate some minerals from the reserve in your system. On the other hand, vitamins are powerless without minerals. Thus it is essential that one receives the necessary amounts of both'.—Dr. John B. Lust.

Vitamins are organic chemical substances, widely distributed in natural foods (fruits and vegetables) that are essential to normal metabolic functions of human beings and lower animals. Only very small amounts are needed but lack of the necessary amount, however small, results in a vitamin deficiency disease (avitaminosis). Among the classical examples of such diseases are rickets, scurvy, beriberi and pellagra.

A Polish chemist, Casimir Funk, invented vitamin in 1911 while trying to extract from rice hulls a chemical substance that would cure beriberi. He thought that he had found an amine chemical vital to life. He had not, but his theory was correct; lack of certain chemical substances caused disease.

Vitamins are distinguished as fat-soluble, notably A, D, E and K, and water-soluble most of the others. Some are heat-labile, destroyed by cooking, notably vitamin C; most are heat-stable.

Taking vitamin pills is not necessary. A good mixed diet of common foods, including protective foods, supplies all the vitamins one needs. Vitamin pills without a good mixed diet will not increase pep and vigour or resistance to disease.

Vitamin supplements are necessary. They are needed when the dietary intake of vitamins is inadequate. This condition often appears in cases of chronic disease, after delivery, after surgical operation, and during pregnancy.

Vitamin needs differ with age and many other factors. Thus vitamin D is much more essential to infants and growing children than to adults. Rarely is only a single vitamin missing from the diet. Most vitamin deficiencies are multiple; therefore vitamin pills and other vitamin preparations prescribed for preventing or treating disease contain a balanced supply of many vitamins.

Vitamin A, once called 'anti-infective vitamin', helps to preserve the integrity of the skin and mucous membranes and other epithelial tissues, making them more conducive to growth of bone and tooth formation. Its deficiency may cause night-blindness, changes in the eye, general weakness, retarded growth, problems of respiratory tract, genito-urinary troubles, gastro-intestinal disorders, and nervous troubles. It is essential to the formation of 'visual purple' rods and cones in the retina of the eyes; its lack causes night-blindness. Vitamin A is found in fish, liver, milk, egg-yolk and in many green fruits and vegetables like garlic, lemon, musumbi, apple, onion, potato, carrot, beet, orange, radish, cucumber, grape, pineapple, parsnip, cauliflower, sweet potato, turnip, brinjal, and in dark green leafy vegetables.

Vitamin B-complex includes a large number of water soluble vitamins like thiamine, riboflavin, niacin, pyridoxine, biotin, pantothenic acid, inositol, folic acid and vitamin B-12.

Thiamine is essential for utilization of carbohydrates and normal appetite and function of the digestive tract. Its deficiency may cause abdominal pains, heart irregularities, muscle tenderness, emotional instability, constipation and irritability. Thiamine is not stored in the body as effectively as many other vitamins; and it is apt to be lacking in the adult diet. Thiamine is often given to restore or improve appetite. Best sources of thiamine are pork and brewer's yeast; it is also found in whole grain, dried peas and beans, liver and egg yolk. Raw fruits and vegetables are also good source of thiamine, especially beet roots, cucumber, brinjal, onion, pumpkin, carrots, spinach, grape, orange peel, and raisin.

Riboflavin is necessary for normal growth and for the integrity of skin tissues and mucous membranes. Lack of riboflavin may cause the lips to sore and show slight fissures at the corners, the tongue to be red and sore, the eyes to itch and be extremely sensitive to light. Milk is the best source of riboflavin; other good sources are liver, kidneys, lean meat and peanut.

Niacin, also called nicotinic acid, is the pellagra-preventive vitamin. Lack of niacin induces the symptoms of pellagra, namely diarrhoea, skin eruptions and mental depression. Other symptoms are loss of appetite, loss of weight, and a sore tongue. Good sources are brewer's yeast, liver, kidney, salmon, lean meat, poultry and eggs. Vegetarian diet is deficient in niacin.

Vitamin B-12 derived from liver appears to increase the formation of red blood cells and has specific usefulness in treating pernicious anaemia. Vitamin B deficiency causes general lassitude, constant tiredness, loss of vitality, slow heart-beat, gastric disorders, beriberi, nervousness, and poor appetite. It is found in asparagus, avocado, beans, beet, cabbage, carrots, cauliflower, lettuce, radish, potatoes, tomato, apples, bananas, grapes, lemons, oranges, pineapple, onions, pumpkins, spinach, grapes, raisins etc.

Vitamin C or ascorbic acid is a delicate vitamin, not well stored in the body and easily destroyed by heat (cooking). It must be replenished daily. It supplies a kind of cementing substance that binds cells together in the blood vessels, teeth, bones and other tissues. Lack of it causes the capillary blood vessels to break rather easily causing bleeding gums, loosened teeth, toothache, gumache, sores in the mouth or tongue, physical weakness, headache, tender joints, scurvy, restlessness, indigestion. The best sources of vitamin C are cabbage, green peas, tomato, lemons, lime, orange, musumbi, beans, carrots, beets, lettuce, raw onions, garlic, apples, bananas, pineapples, cauliflower, pumpkin, pears, papaya, marmelos, turnips etc.

Vitamin D is practically non-existent in fruits and vegetables. It is essentially available in sunlight and for this reason it is known as 'sunshine vitamin'. It is essential to the utilisation of calcium and phosphorus, especially in the formation of bone and teeth. Infants and growing children particularly need this vitamin. Its deficiency causes rickets, poor teeth formation, poor bone formation, convulsions, pigeon breasts, curvature of the spine, retarded growth, constipation, lack of vigour and vitality etc. Adults have little need of vitamin D. When exposed to sunlight, the human body manufactures its own vitamin D. The ultraviolet rays of the sun turn sterols, fatty substances found in the human skin, into vitamin D. Exposure of milk to ultraviolet light produces vitamin D milk. Cod liver oil and other fish oils are excellent sources of vitamin D; so are liver, butter and egg-yolk.

Vitamin E is described as a group of oil-soluble alcohols. Its deficiency causes impotency, miscarriage, loss of hair, sexual frigidity, impaired mentality, sterility, abortion etc. It also develops black and white patches in the skin. Best sources of vitamin E are wheat-germ oil, cottonseed oil, egg-yolks, and beef-liver. It is also found in spinach, watercress, lettuce, celery, parsley, turnip leaves, etc.

Vitamin K is necessary to stop internal bleeding (gastric ulcer). It may be given by injection. This vitamin is available in cabbage, kale, cauliflower, spinach. tomato and in dark green leafy vegetables.

BRIEF NOTES ON MINERALS

Minerals are considered necessary to the nutrition and function of the human body. They are iron, calcium, phosphorus, sulphur, chlorine, sodium, magnesium, iodine, copper, cobalt, manganese, molybdenum and zinc. Collectively they make up 4% to 5% of the body weight. There is enough lime (calcium) in an adult to whitewash a good size basement; enough phosphorus (2 pds) to keep a man in matches for a month; enough iron to make a large nail; enough sodium and chlorine to provide a shaker of table salt.

The mineral elements most likely to be deficient in Indian diet are calcium, iron and iodine. When these three elements are included in adequate amounts in a mixed food from natural sources, the other mineral elements are also normally present.

Calcium and phosphorus are the body's chief framework materials, to keep bone strong and teeth hard and durable. Calcium is essential for blood clotting. It helps to regulate the acid-base balance of the body, the heart beat and the irritability of the neuro-muscular system. The best dietary source of calcium is milk. Other sources are turnip, cabbage, lemons, limes, onions, oranges, rhubarb, spinach, garlic, musumbi, grapes, plums, asparagus, cucumber, radishes, carrots, currants, cauliflower, celery etc. Its deficiency causes mental depression, haemorrhages, trembling of hands, deformities, ugly scars, discharges, headache, dizziness, sour body odour, pessimism, lack of courage etc.

Phosphorus plays a complementary role with calcium. Scarcely any of our vital processes take place without phosphorus. It is available in plenty in cabbage, peas, grapes, carrots, pumkins, cucumbers, raisins, corns, okra, parsley etc. Its deficiency may develop neuralgia, impotency, dislike for work, hard wax in ears, insensibility to pain, dislike for opposite sex, jaundice, bronchitis, paralysis, etc.

Iron is concentrated in the haemoglobin of the blood. Deficiency of iron causes anaemia, fatigue, low vitality and weakness. It also causes deafness, asthma, neuralgia, swollen ankles, bed wetting, defective vision, menstrual pains, insomnia, uterine tumours etc. The best sources of iron are meats, egg-yolk, spinach, lettuce, pears, plums, okra, dandelion leaves, beet roots, beans, grapes, kale, artichokes, black-berries, collards, leek, peas, gram, garlic, radish etc.

Sodium and potassium are another pair of minerals that complement each other's action in the body function. They are largely concerned with water balance. They are found in table salt and other sources are carrots, spinach, apples, garlic, narangi, beets, carrots, radishes, turnips, broccoli, kale, grapes, coconut, pineapple, endive, leek, tomatoes, dandelion, parsley, and artichokes.

Iodine is essential to the functioning of thyroid gland. Deficiency of iodine in the body causes goitre, swelling of feet or toes, enlarged glands, excessive hunger, neuralgic pains in the heart etc. Good sources of iodine are garlic, carrots, beet roots, narangi, lettuce, pineapple, avocado, potato, chives, onions, broccoli, chard, celery, lettuce, kale, cabbage, tomatoes, asparagus and chervil.

FOLKLORE WITH REGARD TO FRUIT JUICE THERAPY

Potato: There was an Irish proverb : Be eating one potato, peeling a second, have a third in your fist and your eye on the fourth.

Spinach: In ancient times, spinach juice was used as a cure for conjunctivitis and defective vision; a cure for anaemia, weakness and low vitality.

Carrot: In medieval times, it was believed that carrot juice improves eye sight; it was also used as a cure for loose teeth, bleeding gums, anaemia, scurvy and rickets.

Beet root: In dark ages, beet juice was used for dissolving fibroid tumours in the uterus, in the bones and in the stomach. Its juice was also used as a cure in fevers, bronchitis, cough and cold.

Tomato: Tomato is neither a vegetable nor a fruit but botanically it is considered a berry. In ancient times, half-ripe tomatoes were used as a remedy for diarrhoea and dysentery. It was also called 'love-apple'.

Cabbage: In ancient times, cabbage juice was used as a cure in gastric or peptic ulcers. Its juice was found to be very useful in all sorts of stomach or liver troubles. For this reason, ancient people ate only boiled cabbage with salt.

Margosa: In dark ages, margosa (neem) leaf juice was used as a cure for fevers, skin diseases and boils.

Holy basil (tulsi): In ancient times, holy basil leaf juice with honey and liquorice was used as an effective remedy in malarial fevers, bronchitis, cough and cold.

Pumpkin: In medieval times, pumpkin seeds were used as a cure for prostate gland disorders, impotency, sterility and leucoderma.

Peppermint: In dark ages, peppermint oil was used as a cure for flatulence, nausea and gastralgia.

Rhubarb (pies): In ancient times, rhubarb root juice was used as a purgative.

Apple: In medieval times, apple juice was regarded as a cure for anaemia, low vitality, and general debility. Ancient people believed in the proverb : An apple a day keeps the doctor away.

Fig (dumur): In ancient times, figs were used as an effective remedy for menorrhagia, diabetes and sore throat.

Anise: In medieval times, the dried seeds of the anise plant were used to relieve flatulence and were considered as a remedy for worms, stomachache, vertigo, giddiness and nausea. They were also used to increase the breast milk of nursing mothers.

Cherry: In ancient times, it was believed that

six cherry kernels a day prevented the formation of kidney stones. It was also used as a cure for appendicitis.

Cloves: In medieval times, the dried, aromatic immature flower buds of the evergreen clove tree were used as a breath sweetener, a comfort for the heart and stomach; a remedy for nausea, colic, flatulence and diarrhoea.

Ginger: In ancient times, raw ginger was used as a breath sweetener; an aid to digestion; a cure for toothache and bleeding gums, and as a strengthening agent for loose teeth and weak eyes.

Black-pepper (kalajira): In medieval times, the black-pepper was used as a cure for toothache. It was also used as a preventive drug in blood dysentery, scarlet fever, small-pox, leprosy, typhus, cholera and plague.

Garlic: Ancient people believed that garlic was a powerful charm against evil eye, demons, witches and vampires. In ancient Rome, the garlic was dedicated to Mars, the god of war. Medieval people used garlic as a cure for heart-attack, cancer and tumour. Garlic was believed to be sure remedy for all sorts of ailments in the body. It was also regarded as 'heal-all' vegetable. Externally garlic juice was applied to insect bites, scorpion stings, and even to dogbites.

In old age, it would be very difficult to keep the body fit and active by drugs. If one takes a few cloves of fried garlic daily and a glass of musumbi juice in the morning, one will remain free from all sorts of diseases. Medical experts gave us this valuable advice.

Onion: In ancient times, onion was used as an effective cure for insomnia, sunstroke, heat-stroke, headache, and travel sickness. Externally its juice was applied to insect bites and scorpion stings.

The ancient people used to eat raw onions at supper time in order to get sound sleep. If anyone eats fried garlic at supper time, he will surely get a very sound sleep.

Bitter-gourd (karela): In ancient times, raw bitter gourd juice was used as an effective remedy for diabetes, eye troubles, jaundice, skin eruptions, liver troubles and stomach disorders.

Lady's finger (dheras, bhindi): In ancient times, raw lady's finger was used as remedy for impotency, sexual frigidity, sterility.

Musumbi (lime): In medieval times, musumbi was regarded as a 'miracle fruit'. They treated this fruit as a 'heal-all' fruit. Musumbi juice was used as a very effective and sure remedy in diarrhoea, dysentery, jaundice, diabetes, cirrhosis of liver and all sorts liver troubles. It was also used as a specific remedy for heart-attack and thrombosis. Musumbi juice was also used as a sure remedy for anaemia, fever, bronchitis, general debility, small-pox, prostate gland disorders, kidney disorders and uterine troubles. Ancient people treated this fruit as all-purpose medicine.

Sabeda: In ancient times, sabeda was used as a cure for anaemia, general debility, low vitality, lassitude, general weakness, headache, and travel sickness. They believed that this fruit was a sure remedy for impotency, sexual sterility, frigidity, etc.

Orange (narangi): In olden days, orange juice was used as an effective remedy for fever, bronchitis, cough and cold, low vitality, lassitude, general debility, anaemia, general weakness, impotency, sterility, kidney disorders and prostate gland disorders.

Lemon (nimbu): In ancient times, lemon was regarded as a miracle fruit. It was used as an effective remedy for diarrhoea, dysentery, jaundice, flatulence, indigestion, dyspepsia, cirrhosis of liver, diabetes, dropsy, and intestinal troubles. It was also used as a cure in eye troubles and kidney disorders.

Plantain (kela): In medieval times, green plantain flower (mocha) juice was treated an effective remedy for menorrhagia. Boiled green plantain was regarded as an effective remedy in diarrhoea and dysentery.

Liquorice (jastimadhu) : In ancient times, liquorice with honey and ginger was used as a powerful remedy in fevers, bronchitis, cough and cold.

Tamarind (imli): In medieval times, ripe tamarind pulp was used as a remedy for loss of memory, bilious vomiting, loss of appetite and travel sickness.

Papaya: In ancient times, ripe papaya was used as an effective remedy for all sorts of stomach troubles. Green papaya was used as a vegetable in diarrhoea and dysentery.

Marmelos: In ancient times, ripe marmelos was used as a cure for diarrhoea and dysentery. A few slices of marmalade of marmelos will be very useful in diarrhoea and dysentery.

CANCER

Cancer is characterised by unwanted, abnormal and lawless growth of cells in the body. A new growth or swelling in the body is called tumour. Usually tumour is of two types, benign and malignant. A malignant tumour ultimately turns into cancer. Cancer cells suck the vital nutrients from the body thereby causing death of the patient.

Classification: Cancer cells can start in any part of the body and each particular part of the body produces a specific and different type of cancer. Carcinoma is cancer of the skin, glands, or membranes; sarcoma is cancer of the bone, muscle, or connective tissue; melanoma is cancer of the pigment cells of the skin; lymphoma is cancer of the lymphatic nodes, and leukaemia is cancer of the blood. Cancer is neither contagious nor communicable. It is also not a hereditary disease. Mostly adults get cancer in their middle and late life. Nowadays children and young people under 21 are also vulnerable.

Causes: Cancer is usually caused by constant consumption of devitalised or adulterated foods. Some doctors have opined that this is a vitamin deficiency disease. Others have expressed the view that it is a disease of malnutrition. Syphilitic lesions of the tongue may lead to cancer of the tongue. Prolonged exposure to sun's rays causes skin cancer. Alcohol taken in excess causes cancer of the larynx and liver. Cigarette smoking appears to be a factor for lung cancer. Chewing betel leaves with tobacco mixture (gundi) causes cancer of the mouth and liver. Excessive or frequent childbirth causes cancer of the uterus. Chewing dried tobacco leaves with lime (chuna) causes cancer of the mouth and stomach.

Warning signals: The American Cancer Association has prescribed six warning signals for cancer

1. A sore that does not heal, particularly about mouth, tongue or lips.
2. A painless lump or thickening in the breast or elsewhere.
3. Bloody discharge from any body opening.
4. Persistent indigestion or difficulty in swallowing.
5. Persistent hoarseness or cough.
6. Any change in the colour or size of a mole or wart.

If these danger signals are heeded and a physician consulted chance of premature death can be greatly minimised.

Treatment: Cancer is treated by three basic and approved methods — surgery, radiation therapy and chemotherapy. Surgery is the oldest method of treating cancer. Surgical removal of the malignant tumour may help to restore normal function of the body, relieve pain and also retard the growth of cancer.

Radiation therapy: For some types of localised cancer, such as those originating in the skin, uterine cervix or larynx, X-ray administered externally can result in complete eradication of the disease without other forms of treatment. Radiation may also be applied to tumours by the internal administration of radio-active materials. Sometimes a radio-active material such as radium is implanted directly in a tumour.

Chemotherapy: It is the attempt to treat cancer with chemicals that might selectively destroy cancer cells or inhibit their growth without seriously harming normal cells. Scientists have developed new drugs like busulfan, chlorambucil, cyclophosphamide and antimetabolites which can be readily used without any side effects.

Hormone treatment: It is another form of chemotherapy. The administration of male or female hormones can produce temporary but drastic improvements in carcinomas of breast and prostate glands.

Fruit juice therapy: An imbalance in the body chemistry and cell metabolism causes degenerative diseases like cancer, arthritis and heart-attack, which can be easily set right by extensive detoxification of the whole body by consuming raw fruit juices in plenty. No other food can give such an effective detoxification of the whole body. It is now a settled fact that dietary factors promote cancer. Constant consumption of adulterated, cooked and devitaminised foods causes all sorts of degenerative diseases like cancer, arthritis, and heart-attack. What we have to do is to change our eating habits. We have to consume fresh fruit and vegetable juices in plenty daily in order to keep our body free from any such degenerative disease.

Dr. Cyril Scott in his book 'Victory over Cancer' has said, 'According to reliable statistics more than 800 people die everyday from cancer in the United States. One out of every five American will eventually have cancer. This killer claims the life of one American every two or one third minutes. Since the year 1900, cancer has risen from 8th position as the cause of death to second place. Heart disease is first and alcoholism is the third.'

From this, you will find that cancer has now become a terror or horror to all of us. No one knows when his turn will come. With regard to its appearance, one famous physician named Gallen gave an wonderul description of it more than 1700 years ago. He said, 'Just as a crab's feet extends from every part of its body so in this disease, the veins are distended, forming a similar figure.' He named the crab-like disease cancer.

C.E. Perkins in his book 'What Price Civilisation' has said, 'There is nothing dramatic or romantic about cancer. It is the result of man's self-indulgence and lack of wisdom. There is considerable drama, however, in the toll cancer is taking of civilised men. Stark gruesome drama, reeking with pathos, sorrow, suffering and despair. What are we going to do about it?' He did not give any clue or hints for its remedy. He simply described the horrible nature of cancer.

Dr. Harry Hoxsey, a herbalist of the United States, first tried to cure cancer patients with herbal medicines and fruit juice. He got the prescription from his late father who was successful in curing cancer of the animals with herbal medicines. Dr. Harry Hoxsey was arrested by the U.S. Govt. and convicted. But his conviction was later quashed as he proved before the judges that cancer of the skin, tongue, face, legs could be cured with herbal medicines and fruit therapy. Judges were satisfied with his treatment and they released him with honour. His main treatment consisted of applying one piece of crushed garlic with a sticking plaster on the affected part and renewing the same after every four hours. He found that cancerous growths of the skin disappeared within a very short time. This is really a remarkable achievement. One most interesting thing was that he kept his patients only on fruit and vegetable juices without any cereals during treatment. This showed that fruit and vegetable juices has miraculous healing powers. He recorded all his observations in his most famous book 'You don't have to die'.

Dr. Max Gerson, a cancer specialist of the U.S., made extensive researches on cancer patients. He observed that cancer was nothing but a degenerative disease. In cancer not only the symptoms but the whole body must be treated. He was convinced that cancer did not require any specific treatment. The main point is that the whole body must be detoxified with raw fruit and vegetable juices. The patients must be kept wholly on raw fruit juice therapy, and they should not be given any cereals to eat. His basic medicines were potassium iodide and fruit and vegetable juices. He has said, 'There is no one drug which can cure cancer and its ultimate conquest will never be made by finding some elusive virus. I gradually came to the conclusion that in a body with normal metabolism, cancer could not develop. The normalisation of the damaged metabolism is therefore essential aim of my therapy'. He also specifically pointed out that normalisation of damaged metabolism could be very effectively done by consuming fruit and vegetable juices.

Dr. E. C. Cowdry in his book 'Trends in Cancer Research' has said, 'One of the chief achievements since 1938 in cancer research is proof that dietary factors influence cancer promotion.' It is now a settled fact that cancer is caused by constant consumption of cooked, dead, devitalised and adulterated foods. It can be easily rectified by only consuming fresh fruit and vegetable juices and no cereals. This is the only specific treatment for cancer.

Dr. J. P. Davidson, a cancer specialist of the U.S., has said, 'Cancer is a disease of malnutrition. It is nothing but a vitamin deficiency disease. What is required is to detoxify the whole body by consuming plenty of fruit and vegetable juices. This is the only key to good health and to save your body from the attack of degenerative diseases'.

Prof. Bauer of the University of Heidelburg has

said, 'We are justified in concluding that nutritive food whatever its nature can protect us from cancer.'

Therefore the basis of all sound treatment goes back to the soil, the producer of our food. What we eat, drink and breathe are adulterated, devitaminised, poisoned by pesticides and food grown in a depleted soil. We are finding it increasingly difficult to obtain fresh air in town and abundant normal living foods in urban shops. What we eat and drink nowadays are largely poison, forced by unnatural methods to grow on depleted soil and further poisoned by insect sprays, traces of which can never be completely removed from the fruits and vegetables, which are often further vitiated by irrational cooking methods. Cooking destroys most of the normal or natural vitamins so that what we eat today is nothing but roughage or poisons. We cannot cure sick people with adulterated or dead foods.

HEART-ATTACK

It is a popular term for an acute failure of the pumping action of the heart, accompanied by lung congestion and the accumulation of fluid in the dependent parts of the body. The symptoms of heart attack include coughing, copious frothy spittle, discomfort when lying down, laboured breathing, rapid heart action, blueness of the skin and lips, swelling of the legs and fatigue. Heart attacks rank first as the cause of death, cancer being second and diabetes third. Men are more prone to heart attacks than women. Heart attacks are not rare in young men between 30 and 35 years of age but beyond 35 years and up to 60, the likelihood of heart-attacks increases sharply. After the age of 60, there is a sharp decrease in the incidence of heart-attacks.

Causes: A major cause of heart failure is coronary thrombosis. In this disorder, a blood clot in one of the small coronary arteries obstructs the delivery of blood to a portion of the heart. If the affected muscle segment dies, the heart may no longer be able to function properly. Other leading causes of heart-attack include severe hypertension (excessively high blood pressure) and obstruction or blocks in one or more of the heart valves. Heart failure may occur within a few minutes after a coronary thrombosis or may develop slowly over several weeks as when a valve is obstructed.

Other causes of heart-attack are obesity, stress, strain, fast living, consumption of more fat and cholesterol containing foods like beef, mutton, bacon, chicken, lobsters, shrimp, oyster, duck, goose, frankfurters, hamburgers, cheese, butter, ghee, dalda, coconut oil etc. Although heart disease is not contagious but it is certainly a hereditary disease like high blood pressure, asthma, iron deficiency, nervous disorders etc.

Fats: Fats are a class of energy rich organic compounds of plant or animal origin which are basic components of animal diets. Fats and oils are primarily compounds of long-chain fatty acids and glycerol. Oils and fats of animal origin include butter, lard, tallow, fish oils, and whale oil. Lard is produced from the melted and strained fat of hogs. Tallow refers to the solid fat of cattle, sheep or horses. Unsaturated fats like til oil, sunflower oil, maize oil, gingeli and raw fruits and vegetable juices possess less cholesterol and less fat and they are often eaten to reduce the danger of coronary thrombosis or arteriosclerosis.

Cholesterol: Cholesterol is a sterol, widely found in highest concentration in nerve and brain tissues. Its high concentration in all nerve tissues suggests that it plays a vital role in nerve conduction. Gall-bladder stones are composed mainly of cholesterol; in fact gall-stones may be more than 90% cholesterol. Deposits of cholesterol are found in the lining of arteries in a group of disease of the blood vessels and heart. These deposits may be quite thick throughout the interior of the arteries and make clot formation more likely. Diseases related to excess cholesterol deposition in the arteries include arteriosclerosis, angina pectoris, myocardial infarction (coronary thrombosis or heart-attack), cerebral vascular disease, stroke and dissecting aortic aneurysm.

It is thought that a reduction in the dietary intake of cholesterol might be helpful in preventing and controlling diseases of the blood vessels. Although the liver produces far more cholesterol than is usually eaten in food, it appears that the dietary cholesterol is more likely to be deposited in the arteries than the endogenous cholesterol. Accordingly some doctors now advise limitation in the intake of high cholesterol containing foods like butter, cream, cheese, mutton, chicken, pork, bacon, hogs, crabs, sprawn, lobster, frankfurters and hamburgers.

Importance of unsaturated fats in the diet: It has been found that the kind and amount of fat in the diet influence the rate at which the body produces cholesterol, the rate at which the cholesterol is deposted and the incidence of heart attacks. In general, these fats that are saturated tend to increase the deposition of cholesterol. Such fats are coconut oil, vegetable oil (dalda), ghee, butter, cream, cheese, beaf, chicken, pork, hogs, shrimp, crab, lobster etc. The unsaturated fats are til oil, maize oil, sunflower oil, gingelly, soyabean oil, peanut oil and raw fruits and vegetables. These fats remain liquid at ice-box temperature and so they do not cause any harm to the body.

It was seen that substituting unsaturated fats for saturated fats lowered the incidence of heart-attacks. Therefore many doctors now recommend the substitution of unsaturated fats for saturated fats in diet. So dietary control is the first and foremost duty in order to check heart-attacks.

Heart rate: The normal heart rate is considered to be about 72 beats per minute. Under stress or vigorous exercise, the heart rate may reach as high as 170 to 180 beats per minute. At birth the heart rate may be up to 160 times a minute but settles down during the first year to about 100 beats a minute.

Heart disease: Heart disease may be of varied types—rheumatic heart disease, syphilitic heart disease, thyrotoxic heart disease, congenital heart disease, septal defects, coarctation of aorta, hypertensive heart disease, transposition of the great arrteries, coronary heart disease etc.

HIGH BLOOD PRESSURE

High blood pressure is consistent elevation of the pressure of the blood pulsating against the walls of the arteries and other blood vessels. Millions of people in India have been found suffering from this dreadful disease. No age is exempt; high blood pressure is seen even in babies. The average age of onset is the early thirties. Heredity appears to be strong factor. Certain types of individuals are more likely to acquire it. Essential hypertension appears more commonly among short, stocky, overweight people and among those who are emotionally tense, easily excited and highly irritable. The nervous, emotional or psychic factors mediated by the endocrine glands are exceedingly important. It is common knowledge that sudden fear, anger, excitement, or other strong emotions can temporarily shoot the blood pressure up. Hidden emotional conflicts have the same effect and are more serious because they persist.

Causes: Although the hereditary, emotional and endocrine factors play a vital role in causing high blood pressure, many other factors may be held responsible for it. Chemical substances manufactured in various body organs may raise blood pressure. Kidneys are held responsible for it. The adrenal and other endocrine glands may be held responsible for raising blood pressure.

Symptoms: Persistent headache is the commonest and most disabling symptom of high blood pressure. Other symptoms are dizziness, or light-headedness, vertigo, easy fatigue and frequent blushing accompanied by rumbling of the bowels; palpitation of the heart and sweating.

Management: Adequate rest and relaxation are essential. Sleeping for as long as 10 hours at night is an excellent habit; blood-pressure is at its lowest during sleep. Mild exercise without competition or fatigue is desirable. A well-balanced diet, low enough in calories to avoid overweight is prescribed. A salt-free diet may be given with good effect. Habituated tea, coffee, liquor and tobacco may be continued in moderation. A diseased kidney may develop high blood pressure. This kidney trouble should be first treated.

Personality patterns: Dr. Lawrence Hinkle, a heart specialist, studied 2,70,000 men to evaluate the role of personality factors identified as striving people, competitive, restless and mobilised. He studied people of different occupation, levels of achievements and education. The study failed to show that men with high levels of responsibility had any greater risk of heart attack than men with lesser responsibility. In conclusion, he found that it affected all sorts of people, high or low, young or old, men or women alike.

Dr. David Cargill in his book 'How to avoid a coronary thrombosis' has expressed the view that animal fats like beef, bacon, mutton, chicken, hog, crab, lobster, shrimp, frankfurters and hamburgers are very harmful to heart patients. Those foods increase the amount of cholesterol in the blood stream and nerves causing frequent deaths from coronary thrombosis.

Dr. Lawrence E. Lamb in his book, 'Your heart and how to live with it' has expressed the same view. He has opined that saturated fats like cream, butter, ghee, cheese, coconut oil, vegetable oil (dalda) increase the cholesterol content of the blood and arteries very sharply causing frequent death from heart attacks. He has advised that unsaturated fats like til oil, sunflower oil, soyabean oil, fresh fruits and vegetables are very helpful for heart patients.

Dr. T. L. Cleave in his book 'Fat consumption and coronary disease' has said, ' The great increase in the incidence of coronary disease in civilised countries during recent times has led to worldwide investigation which have largely resulted in blaming the increase of overuse of saturated fats. The first is that individuals having a congenital difficulty in metabolising fat which results not only in a high blood cholesterol but also invisible deposits of cholesterol in the tendons and elsewhere. They have a very high incidence of coronary atheroma and a very high mortality from coronary thrombosis'.

The American Heart Association has laid down eight point programme for avoiding heart-attacks:

1. Eat less of saturated fats like cream, butter, ghee, dalda, margarine, coconut oil, and animal fats like beef, mutton, chicken, bacon, hog, frankfurters and hamburgers. All saturated fat consumption must be reduced to the minimum.

2. Substitute vegetable oils and other saturated fats by unsaturated ones like til oil, sunflower oil, soyabean oil, gingelly, maize oil, and fresh fruits and vegetables.

3. Use less of food rich in cholesterol. Foods rich in cholesterol contents are beef, mutton, bacon, chicken, oyster, crab, lobster, shrimp, etc and they increase cholesterol content in the blood and nerves very rapidly causing sudden deaths due to stroke. A heart patient can take three eggs per week.

4. If you are overweight, reduce your calorie intake. Obesity is a danger to heart patients. Obese persons are very susceptible to heart-attacks.

5. Start adopting these principles very early in life.

6. Consume fresh fruits and vegetables (juices) in plenty daily in order to detoxify your whole body.

7. Avoid stress and strain, tension, worries and anxieties as far as practicable.

8. Cigarette smoking is directly related to the depletion of vitamin C in the body. Medical research has established the fact that nicotine

increases the heart rate. Everyone knows that vitamin C is a labile substance, easily destroyed by heat and chemicals. Thus vitamin C has got to be recouped daily by consuming fruit and vegetable juices in plenty. Tea or coffee is powerful stimulant to the nerves. While one cup of tea is not likely to create any adverse effect but drinking large amounts may cause irregularities of the heart beat including palpitation or skipped beats.

Crucial hour of heart-attack: Julius Segal and Gay Gaer Luce in their book 'Sleep' have observed that at 10 a.m. a man is very different from what he is at 4 p.m. or at midnight. One of the obvious reasons is the daily temperature which with great regularity rises during the day and falls at night, dropping to its lowest point between the hours of 2 a.m. and 5 a.m. This is the most crucial time, they have stated, when night-workers and railroad people have the most accidents; the time when doctors receive the highest number of telephone calls reporting coronaries. Cyril Fagan in his book 'Astrological Origins' has treated the hours between 2 a.m. and 5 a.m. as the 8th watch (Oktotopos) — the most possible time for heart-attack deaths, as during this time temperature reaches at a very low point during winter months. All sorts of capital punishments like hanging, guillotines, etc. are also given at this time. It has been found that most of births take place at this hour. So this is the most probable time of coming to this world (birth) and also leaving this world (death). It is for this reason our ancient saints and sages have advised us not to sleep at this hour, i.e. 4 a.m. to 5 a.m. It is the proper time for prayers to God — Brahma muhurta.

It is said, 'Muri ar bhunri sabroger guri', i.e. brain and stomach are the roots of all diseases.

The brain and the stomach are the two most important parts of the body which are responsible for causing diseases. If one can keep these two vital parts of the body healthy and active, one will practically remain free from diseases.

ARTHRITIS

It refers to inflammation of joints. It is one of a number of diseases commonly called rheumatism. Arthritis arises from many causes and it is treated in many different ways.

Arthritis has been classified as follows:-

1. Arthritis caused by infection.

2. Arthritis resulting from rheumatic fever.

3. Rheumatoid arthritis.

4. Degenerative arthritis.

5. Arthritis due to joint injuries.

6. Arthritis caused by gout.

7. Arthritis originating from the nervous system. Rheumatoid arthritis and arthritis caused by rheumatic fever are classified as collagen diseases.

Rheumatoid arthritis and degenerative arthritis are the two most common types. Millions of men and women are afflicted with them. But good medical treatment begun early and continued faithfully can often do much to alleviate the pain, crippling and disability.

Rheumatoid arthritis

It is a disease not of the joints but of the whole body, i.e. the connective tissues. This tissue reacts sensitively to substances in the body. Stress and worry make it worse. During rainy season and winter months, pains in the joints become most severe.

Rheumatoid arthritis may appear suddenly or gradually. Fatigue, loss of weight, and poor weight can be early signs. Sometimes it may cause an acute fever and pain, swelling and disability in many joints. Any joint can be involved including those of the spine, but the hands and feet are most commonly affected. There may be vague or fleeting pains in early stages; it may rise in the morning and at the end of the day.

Women appear to be afflicated more than men. Children too can be afflicted. Rheumatoid arthritis usually strikes at early ages unlike other types of arthritis. It appears during winter months. Americans are chronic sufferers from this disease.

Fresh raw fruit and vegetable juices offer an excellent treatment for rheumatoid arthritis. It is believed that garlic, musumbi, orange, carrot and beet juice consumed in plenty may give early cure.

ASTHMA

Bronchial asthma is the most serious allergic disease, and often fatal. The bronchial tubes are narrowed by spasmodic contractions and they secrete an excess of mucus. Hence breathing becomes difficult. The victim wheezes and coughs and feels as if his chest were caught in a vice. An asthmatic attack may last for minutes, hours, or days. The spasm of the bronchial muscles can usually be relieved by adrenalin. Every effort must be made to identify the offending allergen for long-continued asthma can produce serious changes in the lungs.

Orange, garlic, lemon, musumbi (lime), carrot, beet and spinach juice will be very useful.

GLOSSARY OF MEDICAL TERMS

Abortifacient: An agent that promotes abortion.

Alopecia: Partial baldness.

Anodyne: A drug that relieves pain.

Antacid: A drug which neutralises the acidity of gastric juice.

Anthelmintic: A drug that kills intestinal worms.

Antihydriotic: A drug that checks sweating.

Antilithic: A drug which prevents the formation of stone.

Antiperiodic: A drug that checks periodic attacks.

Antiphlogistic: A drug which stops inflammation.

Antipyretic: A drug which checks fever.

Antiscorbutic: A drug which cures scurvy.

Antispasmodic: A drug which checks spasmodic disorders.

Aphrodisiac: A drug which promotes sexual power.

Aromatic: A drug which is fragrant, spicy and mildly stimulant.

Astringent: A drug which checks secretion or bleeding.

Carminative: A drug which prevents flatulence.

Cathartic: A drug which removes constipation.

Cholagogue: A drug which promotes flow of bile.

Diaphoretic: A drug that induces copious perspiration.

Discutient: A drug which cures a tumour.

Diuretic: A drug which increases secretion of urine.

Emetic: A drug which induces vomiting.

Emollient: A drug which stops irritation of the skin, swelling and pain.

Expectorant: A drug which promotes expulsion of mucus from throat and chest.

Febrifuge: An agent used for reducing fever.

Galactagogue: An agent which promotes secretion of milk.

Hepatitis: Inflammation of the liver.

Hydragogue: A drug which causes a discharge of watery fluid.

Lithotriptic: A drug which removes stones formed in the urinary system.

Narcotic: A drug which induces deep sleep.

Nephritis: Inflammation of the kidneys.

Pectoral: A drug which cures pain in the chest.

Prophylactic: An agent which prevents disease.

Refrigerant: A drug which cures fevers.

Rubefacient: A mild counter irritant.

Sialagogue: A drug which promotes salivation.

Sedative: A drug which reduces excitement, irritation and pain.

Soporific: A drug that induces sleep.

Stimulant: Medicine capable of exciting the vital energy.

Tonic: Medicine which sharpens the appetite and promotes strength and vitality in the body.

Urethritis: Inflammation of the urethra.

Vermifuge: A drug which expels worms.

Vesicant: An agent which produces blisters.

Vulnerary: An application for healing wounds.

BIBLIOGRAPHY

1. Theoprastus — *The Enquiry into Plants.*
2. Pliny — *Natural History (37 volumes).*
3. Claudius Galen — *On the art of healing.*
4. Dioskorides — *De Materia Medica.*
5. William Turner — *A new herbal.*
6. John Gerard — *Pardisi in Sole.*
7. John Parkinson — *Herbal.*
8. Nicholas Culpeper — *Complete herbal.*
9. Phillips Miller — *Gardener's dictionary.*
10. John Hill — *Vegetable kingdom (25 vol.)*
11. John Claudius Louden — *The Encylopedia of Plants.*
12. Sir R. N. Chopra — *Indigenous Drugs of India.*
13. K. R. Kirtikar — *Indian medicinal plants.*
14. J. F. Dastur — *Medicinal Plants of India and Pakistan.*
15. Dr. S. K. Jain — *Medicinal Plants.*
16. Bybill Leek — *Book of herbs.*
17. Richard Hyatt — *Chinese Herbal Medicines.*
18. John Tobe — *Proven Herbal Remedies.*
19. Bernard Jenson — *Nature has a remedy.*
20. Nelson Coon — *Using plants for healing.*
21. M. E. Selson — *Plants that heal.*
22. Kristine Nolfi — *My experiences with living food.*
23. Jean Velmet — *Heal yourself with vegetables.*
24. Lloyd H. Harris — *The book of garlic.*
25. W.T. Fernie — *Herbal Remedies.*
26. H. Harold Hume — *Citrus fruits.*

27. Richard Lucas — *Nature's Medicines.*
28. M. A. Grieve — *Modern Herbal.*
29. May Benthal — *Healing power of herbs.*
30. Raymond Berard — *Herbal elixirs of life.*
31. Harrison Dayal — *Ancient Indian energy food.*
32. Charles E. Millspaugh — *American Medicinal Plants.*

***